SIMPLE SPELLS

for

SUCCESS

Also by **BARRIE DOLNICK**

Simple Spells for Love

BARRIE DOLNICK

SIMPLE SPELLS
for
SUCCESS

*Ancient Practices for Creating
Abundance and Prosperity*

HARMONY BOOKS NEW YORK

Published by Harmony Books, a division of Crown Publishers, Inc., 201 East 50th Street, New York, New York 10022.
Member of the Crown Publishing Group.

Random House, Inc. New York, Toronto, London, Sydney, Auckland

Harmony and colophon are trademarks of Crown Publishers, Inc.

Printed in the United States of America.

Design by M. Kristen Bearse

Library of Congress Cataloging-in-Publication
is available upon request.

ISBN 0-517-70338-6

10 9 8 7 6 5 4 3 2 1

First Edition

*In memory of
my father, Lee Dolnick*

ACKNOWLEDGMENTS

My own path to success has been paved by many helpful guides, and I am grateful to all who have shown me how to approach success, both by example and by instruction. It started early.

Thanks to my elementary schoolteachers, George Hanneman and Karen Nelson, for encouraging me in my youth.

Thanks to my sisters, Randy, Amy, and Carol, for believing in the magic.

Thanks to my close friend and stellar example of continuing career success, Cheryl Callan.

Thanks to fellow spiritual explorers and magic raisers Donna Black and Julia Condon.

Great loads of gratitude to Shaye Areheart and Emma Sweeney for adding the elements of their belief, intention, and allowing to my writing career. And thanks to my mother, Sandy Dolnick, who gave me the drive to go for it.

CONTENTS

PREFACE

Every day there are many ways to increase prosperity and abundance in your life. At first you may think it's just a matter of picking the right lottery numbers or getting that sweepstakes entry in on time. After you read this book you'll be better versed in more hands-on, gratifying ways of making your life more abundant.

Don't be squeamish; you won't have to promise your firstborn or give up your personal indulgences. Sometimes getting what you want does require you to make room for it, so you may have to give up the old job to get the better one. With these spells, you'll end up with much more than you started out with. While abundance is both a spiritual and a material state, it is not a Faustian process. You don't have to give up your goodness or your soul to live in the flow of prosperity.

With the right intention and a little magic, you can create abundance and pleasure in every part of your life.

There is only one success—to
spend your life in your own way.
CHRISTOPHER MORLEY

SIMPLE SPELLS

for

SUCCESS

ONE

*Understanding Spells
for Success*

I come to you with a true success story, one that was entirely based on a spell. A woman had worked in advertising for twelve years. She was successful in it, as her title of senior vice president implied, yet she was unhappy and didn't want to stay in that field any longer. Like most people, she worried that she was too old, that she wasn't trained in anything else, that she had no real talent to rely upon. In short, she worried whether it was even possible to make such a vast change. Taking advantage of some ancient wisdom, she cast a spell to change her career. She was a skeptic, but impulsive and hopeful. She didn't know what she wanted to do with her life, but she knew that she needed her work to be more in line with her creativity (whatever *that* was) and to bring her prosperity (she realized that she could easily be creative but starve). It took a while, longer than she liked, in fact, but her career did change. She is a writer and consultant specializing in spell casting. I am describing my own experience to you. I think it worked out well, so far.

Spells are all around you, if you take time to notice them. Preparing for a meeting, you may wear symbols of power or prestige, you may choose a time of day that works in your favor; some people wear a special fragrance or their lucky socks, even "power suits." My mother used to boil cinnamon to make our house seem more welcoming; she was unconsciously casting an atmosphere of energy and warmth. You too are constantly casting spells unconsciously. When you really put awareness behind it, you can make success much more likely.

Success is a relative term, measured and defined differently for everyone. For one person, success can mean making a million dollars, while for another, success is just making ends meet in a crunch. Success is the meeting of a goal, in whatever form it takes. Generally, we are a goal-oriented culture, constantly setting ourselves up to achieve: start a new project, get that promotion, find the right people to work with—the list goes on indefinitely. This book is about using your own power in conjunction with the power of the universe to manifest those goals, whatever they may be.

WHAT IS A SPELL?

For those of you who read my first book, *Simple Spells for Love*, this will be familiar territory. My personal definition is: **A spell is an organized wish that carries with it energy to manifest in reality.**

It's no good just wishing you had a better job and more money—we wish for things every day and sometimes they come true, sometimes not. When you cast a spell, you are making your wish more like a round-trip request. You send it out to the universe with the power to come back to you, the energy to make it come true.

RIGHT ACTION, REALITY, AND SPELLS Spells do *not* conjure things that are not right for you. **Whatever you want to manifest must exist within the realm of possibility and exist within the laws of right action.**

Simply put, spells are strongest for something heartfelt and harm-free.

For instance, Amy was convinced she could be a television personality even though she was constantly told she was too old for the job. Even in the face of all the naysaying, she knew in her heart that she could do it. Determined to succeed, she said she'd try anything, which led her to cast a spell. She knew she'd have to work hard to break through age prejudice, so after her spell was cast, she kept up her job search. Eventually, Amy landed a job as cohost for a local television show. Her wish to be a television personality existed within her heart so strongly, she was able to overcome a considerable barrier.

Your spell must also be cast within the realm of possibility. For instance, if you are an Asian-born émigré to the United States, you will not be able to cast a spell for achieving the presidency of the United States, a post for which you must have been born in the United States. Nor will your spell work if it isn't good for you. My friend Florence comes to mind. She wanted to get her CPA credential, but she hated accounting with a passion. She was just indulging what she thought her father wanted her to do. No amount of magic was going to get her to do something she loathed. I told her not to bother casting a spell to get through the exam. She was better off casting a spell to find the best career choice. A spell wouldn't work because the accounting profession was not life-enhancing and the goal was not in her heart for the right reasons. She ended up in a much more satisfying career and her father was not at all disappointed. It simply wasn't possible for Florence to be a CPA.

NO BLACK MAGIC The spells in this book comply with the greater good. If your goal is in any way detrimental to any form of life, your spell will not work. I provide only safe, life-enhancing spells. This is not *Simple Spells for Revenge,* nor is it a handbook to be selfish and greedy. If you can manifest what you desire without hurting others, you have a good chance at success.

SIMPLE SPELL MECHANICS A spell is a wish that works with nature, the elements of manifestation. These elements are all around you, for they are the basic elements of life, fire, earth, air, and water. In order for anything to be real, it must have the power of these elements.

After you identify your goal, which I call your wish, a spell requires you to gather symbols of each element. For instance, if you were looking for success surrounding a decision, you'd light a blue candle, the flame of the candle representing the fire element while the color blue brings clarity and power of the intellect. You would also have a plant or flowers whose powers would contribute to a right decision; these represent the element of earth. Water, the element of emotions, would be in the vessel that holds the flowers or plant. Your voice, when you say your spell out loud, symbolizes air.

These simple spells are a practice of organizing your desired goals while giving you a chance to participate in creating success. I have interpreted ancient spell ingredients into more modern and accessible symbols of the elements. There is no need for the unsightly bat wing or lizard tail. These symbols—mostly plants, crystals, and herbs—modern as they are, still align natural power with your wish and serve to connect you to universal energy.

IS THIS RATIONAL?

I am always asked how this process works. There is no way of explaining how a few words and symbols can bring about your desired outcome, but it does. It is a nonrational process.

Of course, magic is nonrational. Magic is a way of hooking up your creativity and power to the "chaos" of the universe. While the universe is not a rational place, it holds much more potential and possibility than you could ever imagine. Magic takes you out of a rational, direct route to your goal and puts you in a greater flow, with results you would never have imagined possible.

In order to use spells and create your success, you will have to throw off your need to understand "how" and just rely on your faith that you *can* have some influence in getting what you want. The fairy godmother in *Cinderella* sort of says it all in the Rodgers and Hammerstein lyric: "impossible things are happening every day."

The great inventors and entrepreneurs of our time are our magicians. They will be the first to tell you: you have to take a risk, you have to believe in yourself and your goal, and you have to put aside all the naysayers who have endless stories of why it won't work. The potential for magic rests in your belief that it can happen.

YOUR PERSONAL TOOLS:
BELIEF, INTENTION, AND ALLOWING

You don't have to commit yourself 100 percent to magic. Most of us are skeptical; we're trained to be. Even I have my moments of doubt and I've seen spells work thousands of times.

All you need is a little room for the possibility of magic. The more room you have, the better, but if all you can muster is a tiny suspension of skepticism, it should be enough to work, for a start. Without belief, you're not going to go anywhere. You need to believe in yourself, your goal, and the possibility that you can have some influence in making your goal real. You can always start with tiny steps until, after seeing some results, you feel belief is justified.

If you believe in a greater power, such as God, the universe, *chi* energy, whatever you may call it, you have enough belief to cast a spell. You simply need to move your attention out of everyday life and its complications to the belief that there is some greater energy going on. This faith in an energy greater than our individual egos is what links your wish to the universe, so that magic can happen.

Intention is a little more complicated, especially with success spells. Here you need to have the goal in mind but not too formed or defined. If you believe that willfulness can make things happen, you may have clouded your intention. "Where there's a will, there's a way" does not stand up here. Willfulness can push too hard, going too strongly after a certain goal without allowing enough room for the many paths to where you want to be.

Willfulness arises often because we think we know the

best outcome for what we want. You may think it's cash, but the universe may know that stock options will prove best. You may think it's a summer cabin in the woods, while the universe may be happy to provide you with a year-round chalet. Wealth comes in many forms and intention here is an opening to the many facets of abundance. Believe it or not, we often don't think big enough; we can't imagine all the possibilities, so let the universe think for you. Intend the goal, but don't will the outcome.

Another part of intention relates back to heartfelt desire. I see this a lot in the business world. Many people want to move up in their careers but are ambivalent about the demands of time and stress that come with more responsibility. My friend Peter would complain that he wasn't far enough along in his career at a big fashion house, then describe all the jobs that he could be promoted into as "stress-filled nightmares." I couldn't help but point out that he probably didn't want any of those particular promotions, but perhaps a spell would help him find a more appropriate position where he would feel more satisfied without the additional obligation of stress. Peter's resistance to a promotion at his current job took power out of his spell. When he realized he could work elsewhere, he had much more intention, and his spell worked by opening him up to the many opportunities and promotions available to him at other companies.

Allowing is linked to intention. Allowing is the act of letting it happen without trying to make it happen and without being too hands-off. It is a tricky balance, but you can do it. Your spell needs time to work, but you need to participate, too.

When you cast a spell for finding a new home, you need to allow time for it to work, but you also need to get out there and look at real estate. No spell is going to cause a house to fall into your lap, or on your head, for that matter. You must participate by looking for your home and seeing what the universe comes up with. It's your job to put your physical energy into action, so that you work with the universe to bring the outcome into reality.

Allowing is particularly challenging when you are waiting for much needed funds, like when you have to pay bills. It can be scary—whether you cast a spell or not. Sometimes money or abundance just doesn't come when you think it should. Yet, in all the financial situations where I've seen people on the brink of "ruin," somehow money has shown up, or the people involved have borrowed from resources they've not seen in the past. Sometimes the easiest time to cast a spell and allow it to work is when you feel you literally have nothing to lose. You are often more open to accepting alternative solutions, which usually lead to greater success. Allowing is one of the hardest things about a spell. It requires trust in yourself and in the universe.

If you've got enough belief, if you think you have the right intention, and if you're prepared to allow your spell to work, you're on your way to success.

TIMING IS EVERYTHING

The cycles found in nature are important to spell casting. When you cast a spell working with the energy of a natural cycle, you are likely to get good results. You don't have to remember all of the specifics. Each spell outlines the best day of the week, time of day, and moon cycle for optimum power.

THE MOON The cycle of the moon is extremely relevant to spells for success.

- **When the moon is waxing, that is, when it is growing toward the full moon, it is time to do spells for manifesting, expanding, and growth.**

- **When the moon is shrinking after it has been full, it is best to do spells for diminishing, decreasing, and dissipating.**

There are two weeks every month for each phase. It is best not to judge increasing as "good" and decreasing as "bad," for they both serve our purpose. There are ways to use the decreasing moons to make more abundance. My friend Donna does spells for diminishing debt, for instance.

You are strongly advised to work with the moon cycles. To do otherwise is to waste your energy. Once you accustom yourself to the cycles of the moon, you'll be able to use the energy for more than just spell casting.

DAYS OF THE WEEK The days of the week and times of day also add to the power of your spell. I encourage earnest spell casters to learn the ruler of each day of the week and therefore learn the rhythm of the cycle.

DAY	RULER	MEANING
Sunday	Sun	Healing, Spirituality, Wishes
Monday	Moon	Intuition, Creativity
Tuesday	Mars	Aggression, Passion
Wednesday	Mercury	Communications, Messages
Thursday	Jupiter	Expansiveness, Adventure
Friday	Venus	Money, the Arts, Beauty
Saturday	Saturn	Responsibility, Tasks

I can hardly expect you all to conduct your business or life based on these meanings, but you surely can cast your spells on the correct day for your goal. Once you learn the days' meanings, you may just find yourself using them to your advantage. My friend Bob used to meet with his accountant on Mondays, which is sort of a cloudy, emotional day. He found it was too hard to concentrate. Now he has his financial meetings on Wednesdays, Mercury's day, and he finds that he understands things much better. You may be surprised at your own findings.

TIME OF DAY The hours of the day also carry powers with them, but in spell casting, you're concerned only with the hours of darkness. Before you start imagining Macbeth's witches chanting around a cauldron at midnight, hear me out. **Magic is strongest in the dark because it deals with potential, not reality.**

Spells are messages you send into the care of the unknown that come back to you in the known. When you have broad daylight surrounding you, it is hard to allow for the magnificent breadth of the unknown.

The days of the week and times of the evening are listed for each spell. You can do a spell whenever you please; I present them to you when they are going to carry the maximum power of manifestation.

THE CYCLES OF PROSPERITY

If you have had the privilege of attending a class in economics, you may have been exposed to a model of the business cycle: growth/boom, plateau, recession or depression, then boom/growth. A lot of time and energy goes into plotting our economic cycle and trying to control it.

You don't have to be an economist to plot your own prosperity cycle. The earth's natural cycles of prosperity are shown to us by the seasons: spring (birth), summer (growth), autumn (harvest), and winter (fallow). You simply need to note what your work cycle is. I am a hard worker in spring and fall but not much goes on for me in the winter and summer months. My prosperity seems to follow suit. My friend Joe works very hard in the summer and winter, unlike me. Track your cycle and work with it. Even if you have a steady job and income, look at the time of year you need a vacation, when you're "in debt," like after Christmas, and when you're feeling flush. Again, like the moon cycle, if you work within the flow of your own prosperity cycle, you're likely to get better results.

For those of you who think you're always in a fallow period, read this book and change that. Either you are not acknowledging your cycles or you need to create a new one for yourself; you can adjust your cycle, especially if it is disconnected from your natural flow.

For you who think you want to get rid of your fallow periods and make all time prosperous and harvesting, think again. Each part of the cycle is necessary. Without a fallow time, you could suffer physically from burnout or emotionally from ignoring your inner needs. There's a reason for the psalm "To everything there is a season . . ."; birth, growth, harvest, and rest form a whole. With one piece of the cycle missing, the whole thing collapses. If you don't like fallow periods, you'll be most interested in Chapter Five: Spells to Get Through Inactivity, Reversals, and Lean Times. Even a "nonproductive" period can be full of abundance.

A FEW WORDS ON SPELLS FOR SUCCESS

I am requesting that you reconsider some of your more entrenched views on prosperity in order for you to allow these spells to work their best.

- **Put aside the idea that "there's not enough to go around."**

Your fear that prosperity has some limit to it can keep you from achieving all you desire. We have all been raised with a strong sense of competition and the feeling that if someone else is going for what we want, we might not get it. That is not true. I fall into this trap myself and continually have to remember that there *is* enough to go around. There is enough food on this planet to feed every person; we just don't distribute it very well. There is enough space to provide space for everyone to live; we just don't make it available. Try not to get into the trap of thinking that abundance is limited. This belief will affect your own potential.

- **Everyone is entitled to their heart's desire; there is no such thing as asking for too much.**

Entitlement is an issue we often ignore because it is so buried under the idea of selfishness or avarice. We need to bust that myth. It is not against the flow of the universe or spirit or the greater good for you to have what you want. The sad part is, many of us feel guilty or undeserving. There is some deeply held belief that having everything we want is bad, or once you get everything you want, it will be taken away. In order to truly open up to abundance you have to believe that it is okay to have it, that it is okay to want it, and that everyone is entitled to it.

- **The only value money has is what we believe it can buy (or) money is not an end in itself.**

Our green paper money, as a thing in itself, has no value. Its only value is held in our belief that it can be exchanged for things we want and need. The easiest way to see this is through foreign currency. You get off a plane in France, you change your American dollars to francs, and all of a sudden you have a fistful of pretty colored paper that holds no meaning for you. You have to go along with the belief the French have for their money—that it has value. For me, it might as well be Monopoly money. The value we put in money is a group belief that becomes reality because we all go along with it.

When the belief in the value of money dissipates, as it did after the Civil War with Confederate currency, you're left with a fistful of nothing. It is only as good as we believe it to be. You'll be much better served if you can see abundance beyond money itself and see it in the many forms it takes beyond currency that don't require group belief. You can start by observing abundance as food, shelter, and clothing. The more you observe abundance in its greater sense, that is, beyond money, the more can come to you.

- **Spells do not work for lottery numbers or sweepstakes.**

Most professional spell casters are asked at one time or another if they can lend help to gamblers, bingo players, and those who play the lottery. Isn't it obvious? We'd all be rich if spells worked for games of chance.

Spells that are cast to improve your success work for you in your immediate situation, with all the possibilities that surround *you* in that time. Your spell brings things closer to you, making them more likely to happen.

Games of chance rely on the possibility of a single mini-moment, a very tiny part of time where a number pops up for a lottery or a computer finds a random number in its file. These are not personal possibilities. Rather, they are the very impersonal part of universal chaos; these chances belong to everyone and no one. It is not possible to influence this single micromoment in time to see what will happen, for it is surrounded by infinite possibilities.

Games of chance are part of inexplicable infinity and therefore are not likely to be affected by spells to enhance your personal success.

- **Surrender often precedes a victory.**

Your spells are going to work best when you don't hold onto the outcome too tightly. This is a common problem in spells for success, when the drive for achievement can be so great that you keep a psychic grip on the outcome.

My friend Ali was going for a big promotion at her firm, and all she could visualize was how and when she'd get the job. She did a spell and made a charm for increasing her personal power. I watched her as she kept her eyes fixed on her goal and saw how obsessed she became with it. She couldn't think of anything else. Soon she got burned out on the process, waiting for it to happen, and began to think it just wasn't going to work. She got depressed and started looking for another job because she just wasn't going to stay in the same place now that she had been passed up for a promotion. I can point out here that this process was all in Ali's head; she hadn't received her promotion on her own private timetable and therefore it wasn't going to happen. Needless to say, as soon as she started interviewing, she relaxed her grip and "surrendered" to her so-called failure. Just as she was getting accustomed to the idea that she wasn't going to get what she wanted, it came through.

This situation often arises when we really want something badly. When you cast a spell for something you desire, you amplify the energy around it. If the energy has too much of your will in it, you'll be too attached to it. This keeps it too grounded in our world and prevents the universe from working its magic. As soon as you release your grip, as if you're allowing a balloon to float up in the sky, the universe can shift things around to help it come true.

- **Spells work best when you are objective about the outcome.**

Emotional attachment to the hoped-for outcome can weight down your spell and impede its success. If you cast a spell with great emotional need, such as to prove yourself to someone else, out of anger, in retaliation, or in countless other "negative" emotional states, your spell may not work out well.

When you cast your spell, your emotional state at the time of casting it colors its power. If you cast a spell with an open heart, you'll get good results. However, if you're angry or spiteful, the weight of these emotions will affect what you get. Whatever you put into your spell comes back to you. I always try to cast spells when I'm in a good mood.

Emotional attachment also affects your ability to allow your spell to happen. When you want something so badly you can taste it and you won't entertain any other options or opportunity, you are too emotionally attached. This gives the universe only a tiny portion of potential to play with, since you have created a very narrow playing field. You may get what you ask for, but it may be only a tenth of what it could have been.

• **Part of abundance is generosity.**

In order to fully participate in infinite abundance, you must also experience generosity, or sharing. Since you won't be worried about whether there is enough to go around, you won't find it hard to give something away, or will you?

It is always easier to be generous when you have plenty, but it is more challenging to give away things or money when it seems scarce. You may be familiar with the term "tithing," which is the practice of consistently donating a portion of what you earn. You may give to your church, to a cause, or to an individual (not you). The concept behind this is sharing your bounty, whatever it is, with those less fortunate. You can donate time, rather than money, or things like furniture, clothing, or food. Tithing is an important part of abundance and will be explored in later chapters. For now, suffice it to say that true success is not in having but in sharing.

BEFORE YOU CAST AWAY

Spell casting is meant to be fun and bring pleasure. In any form, it is a life-enhancing process by which you can improve the joy you experience in life.

In other words, don't get too serious. This book is not about business strategy or becoming the best at something. It is about opening up your life to the many diverse aspects of abundance and showing you how to influence and create what you desire.

Also, you are the only person who can measure your own success. Don't compete with the outer world or look for cues of affluence from others. This takes some joy out of creating what you truly want and can lead you off course. You need to find what it is that makes you happy, what your definition of "enough," "plenty," or "too much" is. You don't have to measure success by money or possessions. More and more, success is being defined as living the life you want, whatever makes you happy. That is truly a personal definition.

Cast away and enjoy creating your own abundance, in whatever form it takes.

TWO

Basic Spells for Success

In spell casting, there are always fundamental spells that can be relied upon to create or influence energy in general forms. You don't have to have a specific goal in mind; rather, the idea would be to cast a spell to bring positive results to any endeavor.

You may use these spells as much as you like as long as the moon cycle is appropriate. Some consider these spells introductions to any of the more specific spells in the following chapters.

I would suggest that you try one or two of them before going on to the other spells in the book. These are gentle, life-enhancing beginner spells that could make you more skillful for later efforts.

BEGINNING PROJECTS: OVERCOMING INERTIA

"Start at the beginning." This is one of my favorite statements, because it is deceptively simple. Where is the beginning? As a writer, I can assure you that a blank piece of paper (or a blank computer screen) is daunting to even the most experienced. Sometimes the fear of starting can atrophy the process—or the writer—completely. This is true for almost any project. How many diets are started "tomorrow" because the idea of doing it right now is simply too much to take? Any undertaking, even the most mundane, can be impeded by fear of the unknown, fear of failure, fear of success—you name it. You can invent a fear for almost any reason.

The start of anything comes from the point of inertia, or stillness. If something is in motion, it has already started; the hardest part is in getting that proverbial ball rolling.

To achieve success in anything, you have to start working toward your goal. This means putting out energy, and *starting* something means overcoming the inertia of not doing anything at all. Procrastination is inertia's friend.

THE ART OF PROCRASTINATION You may feel you are a terrific procrastinator. For some people, procrastination provides a way to build up the energy, often fear energy, of NOT getting it done, so much so that they pull it off in the last minute. This works only in some situations and certainly not at all for larger long-term goals.

My friend Sue wanted to lose ten pounds for her college reunion. She put off her diet until the week before. No amount of crash dieting was going to bail her out. One of my clients, John, wanted to make a large career change, but he kept putting off looking for opportunities and meeting people outside of his field. When he got laid off, he used his unemployed time to make his shift, but he regretted that he hadn't started the process sooner, while he was still getting paychecks.

Of course, there's the other side of procrastination, which works often for students. That disagreeable term paper or essay has been known to be a crash effort, after it has been put off for weeks. I myself resorted to that tactic in my school days. I found that the fear of the deadline fueled my ability to focus; the closer the due date, the more likely I was to produce a paper. I don't, by the way, use that tactic for writing books; it wouldn't work.

However, procrastination can also be a sign that you are not ready to proceed toward your goal. If you can't bring yourself to start something, you must examine if it is truly something you want to do. Sometimes we want things that aren't good for us or that we aren't ready for, and putting off actions toward them is an act of unconscious self-preservation. Trudy, an independent executive recruiter, was being courted by a large firm to be their high-salaried human resources manager. Flattered, she had taken the first interview out of curiosity and was supposed to call to schedule another interview with the president of the company. Being in the business, Trudy knew that a timely response was important, particularly to the president of the firm. However, she just didn't make that call. She came to me confused at her own ambivalence and asked for a spell to clear her of procrastination. By the time we had discussed the spell, she had come to the conclusion that she really didn't want the job. Her procrastination was a symptom of not wanting to achieve the goal. She was ultimately relieved and ended up placing the person that company ultimately hired.

Procrastination can also become addictive, particularly when you've used it successfully in the past. Just because it worked once or you "got away with it," you are taking the chance of not achieving your goal if you let procrastination overcome your energy of initiation. It is simply not a productive tool if you want results.

ENERGY MEETS INERTIA: THE BEGINNING The greatest amount of energy you'll ever need is the energy to start. This initiative is not so much physical or mental. It starts with what we call psychic energy.

In the beginning, physical energy has little to do with it. You may believe that the beginning is about having a plan, but I will challenge you to back up even further. The beginning is about developing your psychic energy in order to get to the point of creating a plan or strategy. The beginning is the energetic formation of the goal in the future.

To use the dieting example, the first step would be to make a psychic commitment to the goal, not the process. This means seeing yourself lighter, having reached the weight you want to be. Once you have seen your goal, it is easier to gather the energy it takes to begin the process or the plan. If you can't visualize your goal, you may not be ready to move toward it.

This doesn't mean you have to know everything about where you end up, like what weight you'll be after your diet. It simply means you can imagine the reality of being in the body that is healthy and happy for you. When I cast a spell to change my career, I didn't know what I would end up doing. I just knew the elements I wanted in a dream job: really happy with my work, having my own hours, doing a great variety of work, prosperity. That was the beginning of creating my goal and the energy to achieve it.

The greatest amount of energy you'll ever need is the energy to start. And the best incentive to start is to have a goal that sparks your heart's desire.

Sometimes, however, we don't know what our desire is, and spell casting can be of great help to you here. When you don't know what you want, you cast a spell to find out.

CREATING POSSIBILITIES

Initiating a project can be a multistep process, and you can use many different spells to help you achieve results. You may want to start with a spell to open up your eyes to creative possibilities, then use a different spell to determine the best way to use your creativity. You don't have to have anything specific in mind. You can simply play with creating possibilities.

You may recall in Chapter One that I explained a spell would not work if the goal you desire did not exist in the realm of possibility (e.g., don't try to become Miss America if you're a man). There are obvious roadblocks to some goals you may want. However, **there are many things that you can achieve that you may not even know are possible; they exist outside your conscious possibility but in the realm of unknown possibility.**

Spells are excellent for bringing unknown possibilities into conscious possibility. My friend Karen was an excellent massage therapist and had a large clientele, but she was feeling burned out doing that kind of work. She couldn't even imagine what else she could do with herself to make money aside from waitressing or teaching massage. Cleverly she cast a spell for creating possible new career paths. Her spell included qualities in a job that her current work did not satisfy: more variety, travel, and the ability to do other things, not just one "trade." Like most spells, it worked in a very unpredictable way. Karen took her annual vacation to Europe, where she loved to visit ancient sites. Her travel agent, who had been booking her trips for years, told her there was great need for guides who knew the places Karen had visited. While on her trip, she realized she could guide tours around various places she had been to, and her idea for a new business started forming. Just the excitement of having a new career "incarnation" was enough to pull her through another year of massage therapy while she got set for her now successful business.

Karen did what I encourage all spell casters to do, no matter how long you've been doing it: bring more possibilities into the light so that you have more choice and more opportunities for abundance. Since every choice you make and every action you take creates more and more possibilities, you can keep connected to this flow by doing this spell.

TIME LIMITS Almost everyone I know has a story about a missed opportunity and how hindsight is the only way they see how they could have done something differently or made a different choice that would have led to different results. "If only" is a phrase that makes me very sad. Unfortunately, this is a normal part of life, and no matter how many spells you do, you may not pick up on an opportunity or a choice until it is too late. Even in this situation, take heart; if this outcome is meant to happen, you may well see the opportunity arise again.

Some opportunities have short lifetimes. An offer to buy a house may be "on the table" for only thirty days before it is rescinded. That is an obvious time limit. Some things are less obvious, like when would be the best time to try to move or when to make that big career change. You can't control or perfect a way to make an airtight timetable, but you can use spells to keep you in the flow for what is possible, both in current and future time.

The more you know about your own natural rhythm, the better you'll be at knowing what timing is best for you. The outer world doesn't always agree, by the way. My friend Rose says that the universe often brings you things just before you think you're ready for them.

This brings up the question "What timing is good timing?" You can trust the universe to figure that out. My client Carla always knew she wanted to get out of investment banking but was reluctant to give up a high salary to pursue her dream in furniture importing. The correct timing was shown to her when her firm needed to cut back. Even though she didn't feel "ready," she was courageous enough to accept a termination package that provided her with enough capital to start her dream business. While your magic with the universe does open doors, the leap of faith is ultimately your responsibility.

LEAPS OF FAITH No spell is going to bring 100 percent comfort to any risk you take. You may find that you are still fearful or nervous as the process of your spell takes hold. That is normal. In situations where you are taking a risk, it is important to hold on to a bit of fear to help you stay alert and careful. Taking a risk with blind faith is foolish; you relinquish responsibility but not accountability.

During the spell process, it is normal to have moments of doubt, even panic, but you must allow yourself to feel and then let go of them in order for the spell to work. I see this myself in my own spells. When I worry whether it is going to work or not, I try to use a spell to invoke calm. Worry is completely unproductive and can mess with the energy that you've created with your spell. Look for more on worry in Chapter Four.

PERSONAL POWER REDEFINED

There is a huge difference between power in the traditional corporate sense and power in the sense of spell casting. You may be trained to think that money is power or that a large office, big title, and company car is power. The trappings of power sometimes lead us to believe that a certain person is powerful as an individual. I assure you most emphatically that those things that have become associated with power are not powerful at all, and some people who surround themselves with the trappings of power are not particularly gifted.

Power is not stuff. Real power is personal creativity and the ability to enjoy it. Real power is doing what you want to do and living prosperously with it. Power is not being able to influence others; it is the ability to influence your life. Others, in turn, will be drawn to your power and influenced by it, within their free will and yours.

That is not to say that you can't have the trappings of power if you want them. If part of your creative ideal is to have a huge office, title, and car, go for it; it's all about enjoyment. However, many of us get used to thinking that that is the *only* way to have power, and that is simply not the case. Exercising your power is exercising your free will, your choice to experience what you wish. Real power is the courage and wherewithal to do what you really want.

Often in the traditional corporate scenario and in many real life events, we give our power away. Your boss has the "power" to fire you. Your client has the "power" to say no to you. The guy at the electronics store has the "power" to intimidate me. When things get risky or fearful, it is easy to let go of our own power and to allow others to take over. That's when you give it away. You may compromise yourself, then end up being upset at yourself, and all because you gave too much away. Giving your power away gives others control over you.

My friend Gary used to to go pieces every year when he had to shop for his wife's birthday present. It was important to him to find something romantic and something that she'd keep, not return. Every year he would be intimidated by salespeople to buy things he wasn't sure about, and his wife was usually dissatisfied. She thought it was funny that he turned into a marshmallow in a lingerie store, but he was really upset. Finally I gave him a pep talk and a spell to keep his cool under "pressure," i.e., to increase his personal power. He found success in an antiques store the first time he tried it. He found a little amethyst pin from the turn of the century that his wife just loved. Now he boasts that he can even manage those "froufrou lingerie boutiques." My female friends have used similar spells when shopping for cars and stereos. It can be very satisfying to overcome a once intimidating situation.

Power comes from you. You control how it flows from you and how open you are to its source. You can send your power out into the future, as you do in a spell. You can mask your power if you want to be subtle or you can glamorize it if you want to shine.

You can increase your own sense of personal power through a spell and sometimes in combination with a glamour. A glamour is an energy form you cast over yourself that acts as a protective force or an attractive one, depending on your needs. I'll never forget my first attempt at using this. It was time for my annual raise, and I knew from experience that my employer would never volunteer money; I had to ask for it. I also felt that I deserved a really good raise, if not a bonus, for being particularly productive that year and for taking on a lot more responsibility. At the time, my boss and I did not connect very well—we were on different wavelengths but not hostile toward each other. I used a spell to increase my personal power so that I would not chicken out asking for a substantial raise. I was also advised to cast a glamour around myself so that my boss could see me on his level, as if I was one of his cronies. I literally pulled my hair back, wiped off my lipstick, and sat down in his office in a posture of a man, leaning back, relaxed and buddylike. I expressed my need for more money without flinching, in my most matter-of-fact tone. Damned if I didn't get that raise in less than three minutes! It took much more preparation to go into that room than it did in the actual act of achieving my goal. The art of some spells sets the situation up in advance and then you just move right through it.

I enjoy watching powerful people in public. You can tell who they are because they are at ease in many situations, especially embarrassing ones. A powerful person doesn't worry about what other people think or what he or she may look like to others. A sense of humor is a sign of power, as are patience and the ability to be wrong. Powerful people are complete within themselves. They don't fear much and are certainly not motivated by it.

FEAR IS NOT POWER Power and fear are often thought of as compatible elements, but they are completely at odds with each other. Fear separates people from their potential; it makes it seem easier not to do something than to go for it (e.g., I am so afraid to go to Europe for the first time that I simply won't go and fulfill my desire). If you've ever worked for someone who thinks that motivation by fear is the best way to manage people, you have met a person who doesn't understand power. Keeping people in a fear state does not produce good results. Fear may keep people from doing things to avoid unpleasant results, like losing a job, but it won't motivate them to do their best, even when they are capable of doing it.

Fear creates a wall between you and doing what you really want to do. Fear is hard to overcome, but it is extremely important to learn ways of dissipating it, of softening it enough so that you can move through it.

Don't try to become fearless; that is simply a denial of fear. It really isn't useful, since fear helps us stay alive in dangerous situations. To be truly fearless is not to fear death, suffering, and pain. This is a reckless state and can produce reckless results. You don't have to go that far.

Moving through fear is often very difficult, but can be one of the most satisfying accomplishments. Imagine giving up everything you own to pursue a dream. It isn't easy, for even the most courageous people have moments of doubt. The trick is to convert a wall of fear into a cloud of fear, and to allow it to move through you or you through it. That way, you don't deny it, but you also don't let it stop you.

Fear can also attract the very results you are afraid of, since it is so energetically powerful. Fear acts as a spell sometimes, traveling in advance of the situation, ready to meet you when you get there. If fear exists, as it always does on some level, we have to move through it in order to get to our goal. Conquering your fear usually means you won't have to face that particular bogeyman again.

When Tracy decided to leave college to travel, she knew she'd have to tell her father, a man of formidable temper who had great ambitions for her. She was already on academic probation and knew that it was only a matter of time before her father found out. Tracy envisioned a horrible scene when her grades arrived, with her father storming around threatening her and keeping her from her travels. She just wasn't interested in studying and knew she needed some time off. Rather than wait for what she thought was an inevitable scene, Tracy decided to face her father and her fear of his judgment and temper. She did a spell for releasing fear, then cast a glamour for protection, and met with him on her time and her terms, a weekend at home—in her room, not his den. He was surprised at her news but also upset that she was so unhappy at college. His reaction shocked Tracy, who had expected raging disappointment. Since she had cleared herself of fear, she opened up the space for a different scene to play itself out.

Tracy used a glamour for protection to help her deflect some of her father's anger from her. In her case, the situation was malleable enough for her to shift her father's reaction. However, sometimes you just know you're going to have to face an unpleasant situation and you may not feel that you can influence its outcome. Here, a glamour for protection can help. This is a kind of energetic spell, much like increasing personal power, which simply surrounds you with a protective layer. I often used this in the corporate world when a situation got out of hand. Unlike many other spells, protective energy can be invoked in the thick of things, as long as you remember to do so. Simply practice it a few times in a controlled environment, and then you'll be able to "take it anywhere."

I recall a particularly grueling airport experience, when I got to the airport with only a few minutes to spare and arrived at the gate just as they were going to give away my seat. In the nick of time, I began to board the plane, but not without the interference of a crazed man on standby who screamed at me that I should give him my seat because I was so late. He wouldn't let me past him and his anger came at me full force. The gate agents threatened to call security and hustled me onto the plane. It took some time for me to recover; his anger actually stuck to me so that I shook from his rage for at least an hour. Now I use a veil of protection without hesitation. It is helpful if you are around volatile people and definitely keeps you centered in the face of a storm.

When you cast a spell, you are attempting to influence events in the future. Your spell creates an energy form that actually exists. This is particularly useful when you want to influence the atmosphere of a place where you are going to be or to avoid unconsciously tossing fear into the future.

For instance, if you are going into a room for an important meeting, you can cast a spell to make the energy of the room receptive and relaxed. While this is not always possible if those attending the meeting are hostile, there are great ways to throw energy into the future so that at least you feel at ease in the situation.

Creating energy and sending it into the future is the most basic form of spell casting, so this is not a difficult exercise. In fact, many of us do this unconsciously by visualizing a situation before getting there. Unfortunately, we are exceptionally good at putting fear in the future, but not so skillful at putting calm, spaciousness, and receptivity there. When you think about applying for a mortgage, how often do you imagine "it's a piece of cake" versus how much insecurity you may have with respect to your credit rating or income level? The power of positive thinking isn't just in the mind. You're actually influencing events, if not creating them, when you ponder the future.

Holding on to a goal obsessively also creates a tight hold on future realities. Obsession acts like fear by creating barriers of "how it has to happen," and thereby strangling the possibilities of manifestation. Even if you are convinced that your single-minded determination will see you through to your goal, I beg you to entertain another angle.

You simply don't think big enough.

Hanging on to the goal you imagine is simply not allowing it to manifest in a way that is much bigger.

SPELL BASICS

*If you wish to make up your own spells, this
information can serve as a guide.*

For Initiating Spells

COLOR: Yellow
FLOWER: Carnations
REGARDING CREATIVE WORK: Tuesday
MENTAL WORK: Wednesday
WORK WITH MONEY: Friday
ANY OTHER: Thursday
TIME OF DAY: After dark
TIME OF THE MONTH: Waxing moon

For Clearing or Releasing Spells

COLOR: White
FLOWER: Carnations
DAY OF THE WEEK: Any
TIME OF DAY: After dark
TIME OF THE MONTH: Waning moon

Spell to
GATHER ENERGY OF INITIATION

On any new moon after sunset,
light a white and yellow candle.
Place a vase of carnations
and a bay leaf next to your candles.

SAY ALOUD:

I call in the guardians
and the powers of the elements
to join with me in creating the energy
to move into the flow of creation.
I allow my vision and my heart's desire
to show me the path,
and I affirm I step onto it
with purpose, integrity, and ease.
I release this with gratitude and love
and say so be it.
And so it is.

Allow the candles to burn as long as you like.
(Dispose of the bay leaf and the flowers
after they die.)

Spell to
RELEASE PROCRASTINATION

On a waning moon
on any day of the week,
light a white candle.
Place any flowers you like in a vase with water.
Blow up a balloon of any color, but do not tie it.
Hold the end together so that it does not release
the air.

SAY ALOUD:

I *ask that obstacles within myself*
are released as this balloon releases the air it holds.
With this release also goes fear and distraction
so that I may free the energy for commencement.
I ask that the universe help me in this release,
and I say
so be it,
And so it is.

Let go of the balloon so that the air is released.
Blow out the candle.

Spell for
INCREASING POSSIBILITIES

On a Thursday under a waxing moon
during the second hour of darkness,
light a purple candle
and a green candle.
Place some sage in a natural vessel
(such as a seashell)
and place yellow flowers
(preferably dandelions)
in water, in front of the candles.

SAY ALOUD:

I ask the creativity of the universe
to be shown to me.
I open my eyes and my heart
to potential and inspiration.
I join in the flow of opportunity
and all creation
within the greater good.
I ask that this be done now.
So be it.
And so it is.

Blow out the candles.
(Let the flowers die and then dispose of the sage.)

Spell to
INCREASE PERSONAL POWER

Under a waxing moon on a Tuesday
in the second hour of darkness,
light a yellow candle.
Place red carnations in a vase with water.
Place a piece of raw ginger in front of the candles.

SAY ALOUD:

I call in the guardians and
the power of the universe
to join with me.
With the fire of creative energy
and a sword of compassion,
I increase and manifest my own power
on the plane of reality.
I do this within the greater good
and with respect for the higher order.
I claim this power and say
so be it.
And so it is.

Blow out the candles.
(Dispose of the ginger when the flowers die.)

Spell for
CREATING A GLAMOUR FOR PROTECTION

Sit in a darkened room at any time of day.
Gather your energy in, breathing in a relaxed way.
Close your eyes.
With your imagination,
bring white or yellow light around you.
Let the light glow from your skin,
a shield from the world around you.
Change the color to orange, then pink,
then lavender, then blue.
Feel which color makes you feel safest,
most protected.
Stay with the color you like best.
Wear it as a shield around your whole body.
After you open your eyes,
cast your shield of colored light
around you again.
Invoke your shield anytime, night or day,
in any situation in which you need protection.

Spell for
RELEASING OR SOFTENING FEAR

On a waning moon
on any day of the week but Saturday,
place an ice cube in a bowl next to a white candle.
Place lavender in a natural vessel and
white carnations in a vase with water.

SAY ALOUD:

With the help of the guardians,
God and Goddess,
I ask that my fear gently be lifted from me.
As the ice melts
so does my resistance,
and as the water turns to air
my fear opens to spaciousness.
I ask that this be done with ease
and for the greater good.
And I release this with love and trust
and say
so be it.
And so it is.

Let the bowl remain in place until all the water
has evaporated.
Allow the candle to burn as long as you like.

Spell for
INFLUENCING ENERGY IN THE FUTURE

On a Monday during a waxing moon,
place white roses in a vase with water.
Light a white or a purple candle.
Place some walnuts before the candle.
In a darkened room,
sit before the flames.
Close your eyes.
Envision or imagine the future situation.
Breathe deeply.
With your breath, blow the emotion and the energy
you wish to manifest into that situation.
Feel the energy shift, see the situation ease
with each breath.

SAY ALOUD:

I send this energy into the future
to help manifest the atmosphere of success.
I ask that this be done for the greater good
and within the free will of all.
So be it.
And so it is.

Blow out the candle.
(Throw the walnuts out when the flowers die.)

THREE

Spells to Initiate Successful Ventures

Spell Basics

Spell to Clear the Elements

Spell to Gather Power

Spell to Open
to the Creative Process

Spell to Attract Investors,
Partners, or Helpers

Spell to Attract Money

Spell to Start an Enterprise

Spell to Find a Location

Atmosphere Enhancers

L et's assume that you have successfully diffused any fear or procrastination around heading for your goal. You are ready to start. You have the inner initiative. What now?

Rather than jump onto your path to success, you may want to do a little groundwork first. This is like preparing the land for a planting. Is the soil clear of debris?

CLEARING THE FIELD

The first step in starting an enterprise is to clear the space for it, or till the ground. Sometimes you have a lot to clear out, as if you want to clear a forest in order to plant a field of corn. Other times you're just clearing out the garden of last year's growth and weeds so that you can plant a new garden from the beginning.

This clearing process is a must and is often overlooked when beginning an enterprise. We like to think just forging ahead is going to be enough to start, but when you run into gnarled old roots where your new plants need to grow, you've got problems. This chapter has one all-purpose clearing spell for the purposes of beginning a new venture, but you may want to investigate Chapter Five on fallow times for other ideas about clearing. No matter how much or how often you clear, you can do it forever and not be done. This is because your life and your successes are continuous cycles. Once you've got one thing done, another goal is created. Most of us have many things going on at once, each at different stages. So get used to it. You have to clear away the dead in order for new life to begin, and it can be a refreshing process.

And don't think I can't hear that resistance rising up in

you. If you are especially messy or disorganized, this process could seem like a throwback to your mother making you clean your room. However, I don't care how chaotic your bookshelves are or your closet is. Clearing isn't about neatness. Clearing is a metaphysical or psychic process, so don't bail out.

The process of clearing the way for a new venture follows an elemental checklist. You may remember the elements discussed in Chapter One: fire, earth, air, and water.

FINDING YOUR FIRE Fire is the element of creativity and passion. Clearing the fire element has to do with your creative intensity about your new venture. Are you really into it or are someone else's motives more important? Is this your passion? How much do you relate to your goal?

Kelly was an excellent tennis player, and she enjoyed playing her club's tournaments. She was usually sought after for mixed doubles since she was one of the club's strongest female players. One year she teamed up with a man whom she didn't know too well, and found, to her dismay, that winning was just too important to him. If she made a bad shot or missed a return, he would react negatively and critically in public. She wanted to win, too, but it was supposed to be fun to play and she definitely was not enjoying herself. She tried hard to concentrate on winning and ignoring her boorish partner's remarks, but they were losing nonetheless, often from her errors. Kelly was going to cast a spell for success in the tournament but realized that she just didn't have the energy. This is a classic blockage of the fire element, when the passion for the goal is not strong enough or is being blocked by other circumstances.

CLEARING THE EARTH The earth element has to do with physical reality: money, health, stuff. For Kelly, her earth element was fairly intact. She had her health and her ability to play; she just wasn't playing well.

The earth element needs clearing when we cling to

things that are not necessary or are disruptive to our goal. If your goal is to redecorate your home with a new style, you're going to have to let go of your old stuff. You'd be surprised how many people don't like doing that. If you want to become a long-distance runner, chances are you're going to have to quit smoking. Again, health is an earth element.

The money side of the earth element is loaded with issues for us, since money relates to survival. Almost all of us have fear in this area. No one wants to be destitute. It is much better to address your fears around money than it is to deny them. You may have to invest money in order to make it; you may have to let go of the idea of "how much is enough" so that the optimum amount can occur. The universe has a pretty neat way of teaching you the lessons you don't want to learn, so try to see your way through the money side of an earth clearing.

AIRING OUT The air element embraces intellect, ideas, and concepts. Blockages or old "baggage" in this area are outmoded ideas, old beliefs that no longer serve you. For Kelly, she believed she had to get along with her partner in order to like the game and hence in order to win. She had to change her mind about that.

For businesspeople, air elements can get blocked by drawing from outmoded experience. That is not to say that experience is a bad thing, but its application shifts as times progress. I see this with more senior executives who can get caught in the belief of "I did it this way so you have to as well," which often isn't necessary. There's no need to cling to ideas that don't have relevance to today's culture. I was told that women never got promoted into the higher ranks of the corporate world. That was a belief I did not want to hold on to, since there was a time I wanted to get promoted (and I was). Thank goodness that idea is fast losing its power.

Air is an important element because we stress "mind

over matter" so much. When you believe in something, you are fueling the power it has, but it doesn't mean your belief alone can make it happen. You *do* need the other elements for manifestation.

WATER PURIFICATION Few people like this one, because water has to do with emotions and very few of us want to deal with how we feel about our goal. Feelings run deep and can be complex, just like the element itself.

Kelly had a water blockage, but she wouldn't have known it unless she looked for it. She was angry, and her anger was being expressed in her playing instead of at the object of her anger, her partner. When Kelly realized that she was taking her anger out on the court, she was relieved. She had been getting nervous that she was really losing her touch. Once she claimed her anger, she gathered her courage and spoke to her partner very clearly. She told him to shut up or she'd walk out. That was her choice and her decision. He wanted to win, so it suited his goal to shut up. Once she released her anger, Kelly's passion came back. They did well in the end, placing in the top three.

CLEARING COMBINATIONS When you look at your goal and go through the elements for clearing, you may find, like Kelly, that more than one element is out of whack. That is perfectly normal. The clearing spell can be repeated as often as you like during a waning moon. I use it routinely just so the debris doesn't build up.

I don't want to mislead you into thinking that clearing is always a simple process. It can be, but depending on how deep the roots of an old plant reach, clearing can be arduous. You may experience discomfort, letting go of anger, feeling fear, or just feeling old frustrations. It is hard to predict exactly what will come up for you, but this part of the process is important to your ultimate success.

As with all goals, there is an element of risk involved—the risk of not getting there, the risk of running into problems, the risk of getting more than you bargained for. Risk is not a popular word these days, since we associate risk with putting our safety and our security on the line.

Risk is necessary and actually very healthy. We are constantly taking risks in our lives, but not always consciously. The popularity of bungee jumping not long ago showed the thirst for thrill and risk we harbor. But how many of us take those kinds of risks with our lives for real fulfillment, not just an afternoon's entertainment? Not many.

Taking a real risk, like going after your heart's desire, often seems much more daunting than skydiving. When you really put yourself on the line, you are put into the most potent conscious risk situation—will you get what you want? How will others see you? What will you do if it doesn't work? To most of us, the idea that we might be disappointed is enough to stop us from taking the risk altogether. What if you fail?

The funny thing about going after success in any venture is that there is no failure as long as you pay attention to your results. In other words, you may not get what you want, but you may learn that you didn't want it after all, or that something else that you never considered is now a better road.

For you skeptical readers, you may now be thinking that this is an easy out. It is an out, but it is not an easy one. When I first started to write, I tried to publish magazine articles for a couple of years. The drawerful of rejection letters I have proves I was clearly unsuccessful in this goal. I was rerouted to writing books through this series of failures. Sometimes failure works as a guide to where your success lies.

When people are especially risk averse, I ask them to start slowly by taking small risks. Many of my Wall Street clients are personally risk averse, but they work with enormous impersonal risk every day. For instance, my friend James makes decisions about billions of dollars every day, and knows exactly how much he loses or gains minute by minute, but the idea of taking singing lessons was too much of a risk for him to take on personally. He wanted to sing only because it was fun, but he was intimidated by the idea of singing for a teacher. He started by taking small personal risks instead, so that he could build up to what he really wanted. He started by wearing two different colored socks to work and lived through that. Then he began to take different routes to work, risking being late. He lived through that too. James invented his own risks, enjoying the fact that he could "win" or "get away with" shifting his life and security issues around. Eventually he took singing lessons, and he sure doesn't have a problem singing anymore.

GUMPTION Risk aversion is only one part of not starting off on the road to your goal. The American culture has the pioneer spirit instilled in it, with many words to describe what you need to start: gumption, wherewithal, chutzpah, nerve.

You may not be afraid of risk, but you might be shy of the energy to show yourself as the pioneer that you are. The person who invented the Pet Rock marketed something so improbable yet so successful; that is a great example of gumption.

Many of us have great ideas that we keep safely to ourselves. Fear of failure is part of it, but the simple energy of making an effort to find out if our idea can work is often the missing link.

Now that you're reasonably clear of blockages and obstacles, it is time to call in the power of initiation.

Most of us don't remember that we have resources beyond our own capabilities. When you make that first step, you can access universal energy to go with you. You can send light and illumination and attractiveness into the first action you take toward your goal, no matter how mundane that action may seem. Before you make that first phone call or even before you look up a number in the phone book, you can call in power to bring you to the right number or the right person, or at least to get you off to a good start.

My client Leon used this spell when he was looking to rent a summer cottage in another state. He cast a spell for opening up to the potential of his cottage, for which he wanted to pay only a certain amount. He also wanted his dream place to be on a lake, with privacy and certain amenities, like running water, indoor plumbing, and a decent kitchen. His first phone call, to that state's chamber of commerce, left him dispirited. They didn't have many listings for cottages, but they hooked him up with a county chamber of commerce instead. From there Leon found that most of their listings were beyond his means. Since the power of his spell was still going, however, he didn't even think of giving up. He was telling a friend of his about his frustrations in finding a place to rent and how he didn't know what else to do. His friend happened to know a family who had a cottage in the area who were in need of a house sitter to look after their dog and garden. The place was even beyond Leon's dream cottage, with a deck and fireplace and extra bedrooms, and it was vacant for a good part of the summer. Leon didn't have to pay a cent and his spell worked, typically, in a mysterious but most productive way.

OPENING TO THE CREATIVE PROCESS

If you are looking for success with a new creative enterprise, you may want to cast a spell for opening to the creative process. This is another way of using universal energy to give you the best possible playing field for your creativity.

Facing that blank canvas, paper, or computer screen—or new life—can be daunting even if you know what you want to create. By joining with and giving over to the magic beyond your own knowledge, you can start to get many more ideas.

Opening to the creative process is a way of hooking yourself up to a greater consciousness or universal energy, which has many more ideas and options than you may have in your head. Creativity is one of our greatest non-linear, nonrational gifts, and spells are excellent for enhancing and amplifying your own innate gifts.

Ashley is a graphic designer who wanted to move into the computer world. Her work tended to be humorous and whimsical, and she couldn't envisage how she would fit her talent into computer graphics. Her spell for opening to the creative process took her through many ideas. First, she did illustrations for books and greeting cards. This led her to meet people who were interested in computer games, which she found interesting but not so in line with her natural talent for humor. While she was trying to find a way to work in the game area, she got a call from an old client who wanted to use one of her illustrations as a basis for a screen saver. Ashley leapt onto the idea of making that illustration and others into screen savers that had an element of fun to them, and she has contracted to do several. She opened to the process with the intention of using her creativity in this area, and to this day she is exploring more ways to use it.

Opening to the creative process is a constant mode. We

are always looking for ways to express ourselves and evolving creatively every day we live. Every impression of every moment of every day shifts our unconscious and hence our creativity. Periodically casting spells to open to creativity is a good way to harness this energy.

ATTRACTING PARTNERS, INVESTORS, AND HELPERS

Some projects begin with other people. If this is your first step, you are likely to benefit from the spell to attract good partners.

Attracting people to join with you in your venture is something like a love spell without the need for love. Of course, the best-case scenario for your enterprise would involve a certain degree of love—in the most spacious, nonromantic form of the word. But love is not the objective. In looking for people to work with, you are actually picking a team. Résumés and interviews are decent ways to find a surface connection, but you don't really know if the person is going to be compatible with your work habits, temperament, or value system.

Attracting compatible people with similar values is ultimately the goal for beginning anything new. I used this spell to find assistants back in my advertising days. It took me some time to identify the type of person I was looking for and the skills that were the most important. I realized that truthfulness and loyalty ranked as high as efficiency and common sense. Typing, filing, and phone manners took a backseat, for those skills could be acquired. The better I got at the spell, the better my support staff became.

Even if you are looking for investors you can conjure the energy to attract people with both money and compatibility. This may sound a little far out, since we're all likely to jump on the first person who drives up with a truck full of money. However, you don't have to. Often, when money is needed, we tend to get very nervous and back off from other concerns, like control issues. Then it can blow up. My friend Bryan needed a backer for the graphic design firm he wanted to start, and he was getting very restless working in a big company for other people. He wanted to start his business right away. He was approached by a well-known businessman who had a mixed reputation for his management philosophy, but Bryan saw only the money and not the man. He grabbed the offer, set himself up in business, and has been fighting with his backer ever since. He didn't evaluate this partnership on anything other than money needs.

The worst case is when you sell yourself short. A backer or investor can buy too much control or influence if you aren't clear and compatible in your goals. A spell works wonders here, both to help you calm down and know that a deal will happen, and to find the best person to make that deal with; but it does take that difficult-to-master quality of patience.

My friend Sally was looking for a place to distribute her designs, which were handmade, beautiful but costly upholstery fabrics. She did not feel comfortable approaching large distributors for fear that they would not care enough about her small business and that they would demand exclusivity in all markets. She cast a spell to attract a distributor who would understand the market, would take on only upscale goods, and had the connections with decorators she needed for her business. It took some time, and she was about to reconsider the larger distributors, when she read an article in a trade magazine announcing a new company. It sounded like what she wanted, and subsequently she met with them. The deal she struck was much more in line with her ideal distribution agreement and did not require exclusivity. Furthermore, this deal was a two-year commitment and allowed her a voice in the company's marketing plans. This was beyond Sally's imagination and gave her access to more knowledge of the marketplace.

The deal not only fulfilled her needs but also added to her potential.

The idea of a partnership adding more than just money or support is a new one for most of us. If you give some thought to people you've worked with in the past, some have probably become your friends; perhaps some people touched your lives in a way that had nothing to do with work. I can assure you that anyone who worked with me got to know a bit about spell casting and metaphysics, and I gained "accidental" knowledge in areas like sports, music, and furniture refinishing.

You can create situations that work for your goal in a very life-enhancing and fulfilling way. You can build a team you actually like, care about, and learn from.

I recommend doing a spell for attracting both money and the right partners together. That way, even if you are looking for a mortgage bank, you get a company that works best for you. Even when situations seem impersonal and simply transactional, it's a safe bet to conjure the right people to deal with.

STARTING A BUSINESS OR ENTERPRISE

Now that you've cleared the way and have gathered your power and your partners, if you need them, you're ready to start your enterprise. This is not complicated in the realm of magic.

You are ready to plant your seeds. That is all that is required in this spell. The initiation of a business is the connection of its potential to reality. Like the sperm meeting the egg and making an embryo, you are putting your seed in the ground to make a plant. If you've done the work in clearing, your plant should grow quite well (unless you are planting during a fallow time).

This spell is a ritual that you do unconsciously every

time you plant things in the earth or in a pot. It is really that simple.

Believe it or not, I have met people who "hate" plants. They resist this spell most aggressively. I don't have an answer to this resistance except to offer a clearing spell to dissipate the hatred. If you happen to fall into this category, please take a look at why you hate plants. They are absolutely necessary to life. Your resistance will affect the growth not only of your plant but of your enterprise.

FINDING A LOCATION

My experience with using spells to find property is extensive. In the earlier example, just by opening to the process, Leon found his dream rental cottage. I have found apartments this way, and many of my clients used this spell successfully.

The most important contribution you can make to location conjuring is patience and surrender, two of the most difficult traits to muster. When you are looking for location, whether for living, working, or temporary purposes, you need to look for it and to trust that it will come to you, a tricky balance of your influence and divine intervention.

My last apartment experience was the perfect exercise in balance. The spell involves visualizing the atmosphere of the place you want to find and also giving some description; for me it was an elevator building, close to greenery (since I live in New York City, this is a special order), spacious, light, and under $900 per month. I also asked for my place to be surrounded by beauty, which to me meant that it would look beautiful. As required, I looked in the papers, saw apartments by the dozen, and was virtually laughed at when I told brokers how much money I wanted to spend. The kind of place I wanted was typically over $1,300 per month. I gave up after driving myself and my friends crazy with my anxiety. I figured I would just make do with my current place, an $1,100-per-month walk-up. I was depressed, but at least I had stopped being anxious.

Only a day or two later, I walked down a street bordering a park and noticed an apartment building with an old sign saying ELEVATOR APARTMENTS. On a whim, I decided to ring the super's bell and ask if there were apartments available. In less than a day I found myself signing a lease to a large apartment that cost exactly $899.59. I knew my spell had worked. After moving in I also noticed a bit of divine humor: outside of my bedroom window hung a large old sign that read BEAUTY SCHOOL—surrounded by beauty! Yes, that's the universe for you. I just wished I had asked for a dishwasher.

ATMOSPHERE As you start your enterprise, you can do a compatible spell for developing an atmosphere you would like to work in. Some people like cool, calm atmospheres, while others love energetic, colorful moods. You can choose what you want, or if you are undecided, you can request that the universe send you the right atmosphere for a successful venture. Given the way some offices look today, this is a highly underused tactic.

There are many atmospheric cues when you enter a business. Colors, flowers, the lines of architecture, even type of furniture and its age affect the energy of a room. I am always telling people to put lavender in the corners of rooms when they want calmness and serenity. I advise against red roses for any business purposes, unless your venture has something to do with romantic passions.

Clearing energy is also an important part of atmosphere, and you will benefit by doing this if you are moving into a new space. Just burning a bit of sage or placing an onyx in a room can clear or absorb negativity that could affect both you and people who enter your space. Why take the chance?

You've been asked to pay attention to your personal energy cycle: when your work energy is at its strongest versus when you are generally tired or distracted. When you start an enterprise, it is best to hook onto the beginning of your work cycle, even if it is contraseasonal.

Frank, a former client, wanted to open a nursery for both indoor and outdoor garden plants in a busy metropolitan area. He had envisioned starting it off in spring, when the public is "thinking" about flowers and plants. Spring, however, has never been Frank's best season. He has taken his vacations in March and April for ten years; it was going to be a hard habit to break.

Frank's cycle usually picked up in midsummer and he was quite enthusiastic in the fall. Yet he simply could not imagine opening a nursery in the heat of the summer when everyone had already planted their gardens. He felt more comfortable in trying to shift his own cycle. Since his financing was in place and he already owned the location, he had the luxury of choosing his starting date. He fixed on opening in the spring, but he found that by February, his energy was dragging with every phone call he had to make and every problem or snafu he had to face. Resigned to postpone his opening, he went on vacation in March. His nursery opened in June, and though slow in building, his business was thriving by August and all through the autumn. He had the energy to make it work and the time to get it thoroughly together instead of going against his inner timing by force.

STRANGE SIDE EFFECTS

Sometimes spells encompass different goals and energies, as if you cast a spell for one thing and it ends up affecting more than one outcome. This is a common side effect to larger-scale spells, like these for initiating ventures.

Believe it or not, one side effect is pregnancy. In metaphysics, creating a new life is the same as creating a new project, although most of us would agree that children are by far the most important creative project we could ever initiate. When you develop a fertile playing field for your new project, you may also be opening up to a new life. If you are of childbearing age, please be conscious of this side effect. Pay attention to unconscious needs for children and of course to your responsibility in birth control. It is hard enough to nurture a new enterprise without having to wake up every two hours for feedings!

Another side effect of these initiating spells is the unpredictability of their outcomes. You'll get results, but you probably won't get exactly what you envisioned. That's why you use magic—to open up the possibilities. You may think you just want to run a little cottage industry, but the universe may want you to be an industry leader. Conversely, you may think you want to be a high-powered executive but instead find true happiness in self-employment. The only one to judge your success is you, and if you are happy and comfortable at this point of the initiation process, you probably won't be disappointed.

SPELL BASICS

Depending on what kind of venture you are initiating,
you can choose different basics.
You can use the spells in this chapter
to identify which color or day is best
for the spell you wish to create.

COLOR: Green or yellow
FLOWER: Yellow flowers
DAY OF THE WEEK: Friday or Sunday
TIME OF THE MONTH: Waxing moon
HERBS: Chamomile, cinnamon, ginger

Spell to
CLEAR THE ELEMENTS

After sunset during a waning moon,
light a white candle.
Place white flowers in a vase with water.
In a natural vessel (such as a seashell)
place
nutmeg,
cinnamon
chamomile,
rose petals.

SAY ALOUD:

I call in the elements of life,
fire, earth, air, and water,
and ask that the path
to my success be gently cleared.
I allow myself to open to this process
with trust and faith.
So be it.
And so it is.

Let the candle burn for an hour.
(Dispose of the herbs before the new moon.)

Spell to
GATHER POWER

On a Tuesday during a waxing moon
and in the second hour after sunset,
light a yellow candle.
Place yellow flowers in a vase with water.
Place fresh gingerroot next to the flowers.

SAY ALOUD:

I call in the elements and the guardians.
The power of the universe joins with me
to expand and enhance
my connection.
I open to my power in all forms
within all possibility.
With the greater good, I ask that this be done.
So be it.
And so it is.

Let the candle burn as long as you like.
(Dispose of the gingerroot on the full moon.)

Spell to
OPEN TO THE CREATIVE PROCESS

On a Friday during a waxing moon
and in the first hour after sunset,
light a green candle.
Place yellow roses in a vase with water.
Place caraway seeds and cinnamon
in a natural vessel.

SAY ALOUD:

*With the power of the elements
and the connection to universal creativity,
I open my consciousness to the creative flow.
The bounty of ideas and resources
opens to me with ease and joy.
I allow all possibilities to be seen.
I ask that this be done for the greater good.
So be it.
And so it is.*

Blow out the candle and relight it when
you are in need of a creative boost.
(Dispose of the herbs on the full moon.)

Spell to
ATTRACT INVESTORS, PARTNERS, OR HELPERS

On a Friday during a waxing moon
and in the third hour of sunset,
light a green candle.
Place yellow roses in a vase with water.
Place chamomile in a natural vessel
next to the roses.

SAY ALOUD:

With the blessing of Venus
and the power of the elements,
I open to people of like mind, heart, and passion
to contribute to the manifestation of success.
I affirm I am open to all appropriate possibilities
and that I choose with clarity and trust.
I ask that this be done within the greater good.
So be it.
And so it is.

Blow out the candle.
Carry the chamomile with you
when you meet with new prospects.

Spell to
ATTRACT MONEY

On a Friday during a waxing moon and
in the second hour after sunset,
light a green candle.
Place yellow roses in a vase with water.
Dab one of the following scents on the candle:
poppy,
honeysuckle,
almond.
Place a bunch of grapes next to the candle.

SAY ALOUD:

*I draw in the eternal flow of prosperity
to connect with me on this Venus evening.
I call in fire, earth, air, and water
to manifest abundance around me.
I affirm I am open to all forms of prosperity,
and that it comes to me easily and readily.
I ask that I be guided to use this gift
within the greater good.
So be it.
And so it is.*

Blow out the candle. Eat at least one grape.
You may repeat this spell on any day
during a waxing moon hereafter.

Spell to
START AN ENTERPRISE

On a Sunday during a waxing moon
in the first hour
after sunset,
light a green candle.
Place seeds for any plant in a pot of soil.
Place a glass of water next to the pot.

SAY ALOUD:

With the power of the universe
and the elements,
I initiate my new enterprise.
I plant these seeds as my project takes root.
I grow this life as my creativity becomes a reality.
I affirm that I encourage and participate in growth.
And I ask that divine power and free will
guide me within the greater good.
So be it.
And so it is.

Water the plant. Blow out the candle.
Look after the seeds.
When and if they sprout through the soil,
your spell is done.
Keep the plant or give it to someone
who will care for it.

Spell to
FIND A LOCATION

On a Sunday during a waxing moon
and in the fourth hour of darkness,
light a green candle and an orange candle.
Next to the candles, place a vase
with your favorite flowers.
Place an onion, carrot, or potato next to the flowers.
Make a list of all the aspects you want
in your location: atmosphere, security,
convenience, cost, size.

SAY ALOUD:

*I call in the elements and the power of the universe
to join with me in attracting the right location
for my needs.
I participate in this process with trust and action.*

Close your eyes. Visualize your location. Breathe it.
Feel it. Be in it. Read your list aloud.

SAY ALOUD:

*Within the right action, I ask that this be done.
So be it.
And so it is.*

Let the candles burn as long as you like.
Use the root vegetable in cooking
before the full moon.

ATMOSPHERE ENHANCERS

*Use these scents, plants, or crystals in a room
to create an atmosphere you desire.*

For openness, ease, spaciousness:
lavender, olive gardenia, violet,
rose quartz, amethyst.

To diminish negativity:
onyx, citrine, basil, sage.

To amplify energy and creativity:
cinnamon, ginseng, garnet, opal.

To give courage and clarity:
sweetpea, yarrow, lily of the valley,
clear quartz crystal.

FOUR

Spells to Enhance Ongoing Enterprises

Spell Basics

Spell for Continued Growth

*Spell for Spaciousness
for Growth and Increasing Potential*

*Spell to Create a
Positive Personal Atmosphere*

Spell to Increase Staying Power

Spell for Ease in Management

Spell for a Psychic Anchor

Spell for Clarity

Spell for Gratitude

Success is a multilayered process. Many goals come in pieces; first, you get started, that can be your first successful sign. Then partners join you or you make contact with someone who supports you in your goal. Again, that is a piece of success. This keeps going even after you arrive at your so-called goal—you may want to maintain it or keep going from there. Success is not an end in itself. Rather, success is an ongoing process that you define and redefine every step of the way.

If your project or goal is well underway by now, it may be time to look at maintaining growth, boosting the energy, or just taking a hands-off approach.

MAINTAINING GROWTH

Looking after your task or goal requires certain nurturing qualities. This does imply a more feminine, caretaking energy than the masculine, manifesting energy you used to initiate your goal. After gathering all the force to overcome inertia and really be on your way, it is time to ease up a little and accustom yourself to a different rhythm.

When a new plant has broken through the soil's surface, there is only so much you can do to make it grow. While many of us are inclined to go and pull on the shoots to hurry the process up, it won't work. What is needed are periodic checks for weeds, water, and trouble from pests. It is now your responsibility to guide your plant or project so that it can take its fullest, most healthy form. Again, there is a balance between irrigation and overwatering. You need to find what's right for you.

Hugh started his own graphic design shop after leaving a career as an advertising art director. He gathered the money, found the space for his studio, and attracted a handful of clients. His beginning was very successful. But after a year, his business was pretty much in the same state: enough clients to pay the bills but no real growth. Hugh was frustrated. He wasn't sure what his next move should be; he'd tried mailers to attract new business, but they were costly and had not paid off. Hugh performed a spell to help his business grow. He didn't have the first clue what to do, so he was very open for the spell to work. Like many spells, it worked in a surprising way. Hugh lost an account, a labor-intensive travel agency that was one of his first accounts. Hugh got nervous and thought that his spell might have gone bad. Within a week the situation had reversed itself. Another travel agency Hugh had contacted signed up with him. This account was much more lucrative than the first.

Hugh's spell worked on two levels—it cleared the "weed" and brought in a much bigger plant. Occasionally, a spell can have that effect, particularly if you are open to it.

SPACIOUSNESS FOR GROWTH Another type of nurturing occurs when you allow your project to take its own course, in its own time. In dieting, for instance, you can't weigh yourself every day because you are unlikely to see any effect. Yet when you check your progress once a week, you may have the satisfaction of tangible results.

In these situations, we need spaciousness. This means creating space in yourself and your project to allow it to come to its fullest form. Spaciousness is not dissimilar to clearing spells, but instead of clearing the field, you are making the field larger.

Annie had an independent film project she was in the midst of producing. All of the elements had come together: director, actors, script, editing. The film was basically done, but not yet seen by the public. Annie had an inkling that the film could be a great success, but she didn't know how she could make that happen. She cast a spell for spaciousness, to allow the project to grow to its fullest potential, and let it go.

When the film was in its final "polishing off" stage, Annie was contacted by a magazine interested in doing an article on the film. Then several film festivals asked to hold the film's debut and a cable TV network wanted to pick up the film's TV rights. Annie felt that the potential for people seeing the film had been greatly increased, and she credited her spell for this effect.

You may be interested to know that spells for spaciousness for growth can be used on even the most mundane things. I have friends who use them to make their gardens and houseplants grow!

REVITALIZING THE ENERGY

There are times when ongoing enterprises need a boost or some sort of nourishment. You may need to plow money or energy back into your project just to keep it well fed.

If you do a spell for spaciousness and want to boost the energy of manifestation alongside it, you can reapply the spell to start a successful enterprise, as detailed in the previous chapter. There is no harm in doing this spell as long as you don't obsess or hold on to expectations. Do the spell, let it go, and see how it manifests. Additionally, you do need to perform some sort of tangible effort that represents conscious fertilization of your project. For instance, if you are trying to encourage a business to grow, you will need to do some sort of outer-world or real-world task that shows you are serious. Here's where some sort of publicity campaign or open house may draw new prospects. If you're trying to buy a house, you may want to look in new places, or if you're trying to sell a house, you could try listing with a new broker or running another ad. In some cases, just buying office supplies or fresh flowers is enough of an effort.

Fertilizing the energy to success is a nice way of keeping in touch with your progress and revitalizing your own power and participation. As long as you do it with the intention to let your goal take its most healthy form and not keep the energy too narrow, you'll find pleasant results.

ENERGETIC MANAGEMENT PRACTICES Wouldn't it be ideal to simply walk into a room and be able to manipulate the people in it to behave as you wished? Forget it. The fun of magic is playing with it in the realm of free will, where everyone has a choice in how they respond. You can see how powerful you are by how much you actually can influence others and outcomes. You'll be surprised how much natural opportunity exists. It wouldn't be any fun if you could always have your own way, no matter what you think.

Managing others is something we do in all our relationships. We manage our in-laws, we manage a housekeeper, we manage the people we work with. Managing others is really managing ourselves, and once you understand that, you can start making some real progress.

PERSONAL ATMOSPHERE **People respond to your energy more often than to the words that come out of your mouth.**
I used to work with a man whom I didn't like a whole lot. Looking back, I guess he sensed this because he always apologized whenever he talked to me or had to ask me for something. I couldn't stand it and I took to saying no to him just to punish him for being so pathetic. (This was before I became skillful at magic management.) Of course, my hostility only prompted him to apologize more. It was an obvious problem and it was mine, not his.

Eventually I took a different tack. I did a spell to ease up my own personal atmosphere so that, even if I was irritated, I wouldn't put out such negative energy. I couldn't get over my judgment about this guy and why I didn't like him, but my spell did work; rather than get annoyed, I shifted into an efficiency mode—I just wanted to get the job done. My energy was less emotionally charged. This opened up the comfort zone for both of us, and soon his apologies became less necessary. Then they stopped altogether. He stopped being afraid of me when I stopped putting out the energy of dislike and irritation.

Let's go back to that room full of people for a moment. You are walking into a gathering of some sort where you don't know anybody, but you are expected to speak, assert an opinion, or somehow put yourself forward. How are you going to do it? If you are afraid of public speaking, as most people are, you are already at a disadvantage. If you are not absolutely sure how to say what you want to, you are not in a strong position either. A series of spells can make you more comfortable with this situation. Hopefully, since you've probably been warned that you are going into this situation, you've thrown energy into the future to make the room spacious and relaxed, or at least receptive to your energy. Also, you may have cast a spell to increase your personal power and perhaps you've made a charm to carry with you. If you've done this already, you're in great shape. All you need to do is to cast one more spell, like a relationship spell. This spell is for smooth interpersonal relations, which means it affects you and other people. I call this the spell for ease in management.

My friend Jane, a young talent agent, was putting together a deal for one of her clients. She was dealing with what she called "heavy hitters," men with years of experience and reputations for tough negotiating. Her past experience with them had been unpleasant: she could hardly get a word in edgewise and no one would listen to her. To shift the energy to her side, Jane cast a spell for management ease. She was, however, prepared for a full-blown fight in order to get what she felt her client deserved in the deal.

On the day of the meeting, Jane carried with her a

charm for personal power and a certain optimism that her spell was going to work. She walked into the room and found all the executives assembled. She took her place and sat back. She waited for someone else to start the meeting. Eventually, the conversation started and everyone got down to business. Jane didn't take an aggressive stance; instead, she was very laid-back until someone directed a question to her. Jane participated only when her end of the deal was discussed, and even then, she kept her words simple and her tone even. Eventually, when she put her terms before the others, they were accepted without much resistance. Jane was surprised. She hadn't put half the energy she had been anticipating into the negotiations. Afterward, she realized that she had been more focused than she had been in other meetings and she hadn't allowed herself to get distracted by other people's arguments. Nor had she been intimidated by her own idea of heavy hitters. Jane's spell gave her a much more pleasant experience as well as her desired outcome.

Management spells aren't just for special occasions. You can use them any time you want to ease the energy between you and others. They are best used in situations where you are not emotionally immersed in the people involved, not with your family or loved ones. These spells increase your objectivity, and when you are emotionally involved you are not objective, no matter what you say. Spells for easing personal relationships are similar but somewhat more gentle.

STAYING POWER In your process with your ongoing enterprise, you may find yourself exasperated, frustrated, or even bored. This is natural, considering that you may want things to happen more quickly than they do or would prefer more participation in the process than is appropriate.

We are all somewhat addicted to excitement, and when things are going smoothly, we may get restless. This is a dangerous state, since we can create crises by our own need for something to do. Most of us have experienced dramatic problems in our lives, and while they are often unpleasant experiences, they do lead to resolution, relief, and sometimes even gratification. Unconsciously, we can create problems just to stir things up and to have the satisfaction of resolving them.

My friend Trent, an artist, continually puts himself through crises when he is in the process of working. Particularly if he has a big show coming up, he falls into a cycle of intense work energy followed by a well of self-doubt and then a block, so that he can't work for a few days, sometimes even a week. I've watched him create this cycle year after year, and eventually I offered him a spell to relieve him of what seemed to me an unnecessarily tiresome habit. He was surprised at my point of view; to him, artists were supposed to go through that intensity of work and doubt. He felt it made him a better painter. I must say I was amused at his response, but since he felt his cycle was crucial to his artistic mode, I let it be. The point is, it doesn't have to be; you can do your work in whatever form you choose.

You can choose to create an atmosphere of serenity, tranquillity, and balance in your work. You may find that you resist it, however, if you are convinced that crisis management is the only way you can get things done. If you feel that you are addicted to crises, it would probably be best for you to do a clearing spell before you invoke ease in management and staying power. There is no point in creating tranquillity if you think it precludes you from being successful.

For those of you who are looking for ways to keep yourself busy without creating crises, you have a number of practical options. You can paint the walls of your space, particularly if you choose a color that enhances your mood or the feeling of your enterprise. You can add plants, also with a focus on the kind of plants that add to the feeling of energy or vitality you want. I also suggest changing furniture around. This shifts energy both physically and psychically, which can give you a sense of movement and renewal.

If your goal has nothing to do with a physical space, you can divert your attention away from worrying yourself into a crisis by taking more practical steps within yourself. Read books to add to your knowledge about your interest. Talk to people with similar experience and compare tactics or ideas. In short, distract yourself with goal-enhancing tasks that can add to your individual experience without inflicting unnecessary, problem-causing energy onto your goal.

Staying power is linked to the notion of tranquillity. It requires you to be patient with the process of your enterprise while maintaining belief and optimism. Staying power is much easier to attain when you create the energetic opportunity for space and change within yourself. It is rather like opening your goal to its fullest potential, but instead of concentrating on your goal, you are focusing on yourself.

WORRY NOT

Worry is the most unnecessary mental state that you can summon, and we all do it with great finesse. Worry seems to be the anxiety of choice when we have time on our hands and no idea where to put it. **Worry is completely nonproductive.** So, take a tally on how much you do it and how much you rely on it in your daily routine.

Like crises, worry can be addictive. My client Gina actually believed that if she worried hard enough, whatever she was worried about could be averted. At the beginning of this book, we saw how obsession can strangle the energy out of your wish as well as create a fear that comes true in the future.

I am certainly not expecting you to stop worrying from this moment on. You can't, but you can start to use some of these spells to relieve you of overworrying or obsessing. Again, you need to conjure space within yourself in order to go beyond the point of worry. You can always try the rational process first, which is the stack of questions that follows:

- Is what I am worried about going to make me die?
- Is what I am worried about going to leave me penniless?
- Is what I am worried about going to leave me homeless?

If you answer no to the above questions, you're in good shape. It is reasonable to worry if your basic survival needs are at stake. That, in any case, is justifiable fear and will help you to make careful decisions. However, if you are just worried about the outcome you desire (i.e., will this deal work out, will I reach my goal, am I going to be a failure), you are likely to inflict too much negativity onto your project.

Spells for spaciousness help, to a certain extent. They can unhook your unconscious need to worry so that you can use your energy more productively. You can also use a psychic anchor to train you out of a worried state.

PSYCHIC ANCHORS Used often for retraining people out of negative behavior patterns, psychic anchors add power to behavior modification processes. Psychic anchors are literally gestures that invoke the feeling you want. For instance, putting your hand on your heart can be a gesture or psychic anchor to help you relax. I often put my hand on my forehead to calm down when I'm getting too excited. These gestures are not powerful in themselves. You make them up in a spell format and anchor the feeling with a gesture.

My client Haley was completely cool and self-assured until she had to travel on business. She worried nonstop when she had to fly to a strange city. She kept her travel to a minimum, but she couldn't always avoid it. Haley's doctor gave her a prescription for tranquilizers, but she didn't like to have to rely on a drug for a self-imposed worry. It wasn't a fear of flying, it was just that once in the air, she worried about being on time, getting to the car rental place, driving out of the airport—everything. She came to me for advice and I led her through a spell to create a psychic anchor. She found that rubbing her abdomen comforted her; it reminded her of when her grandmother would rub her tummy when she was little. She "anchored" the feeling of comfort and security there. Armed with her pills and her spell, she went to the airport not long after for a business trip. She kept her pills within reach but didn't need them in the end. She walked onto that plane rubbing her tummy and rubbed it pretty much every few minutes through her short flight. She was thrilled to invoke a feeling of calm where she used to only feel anxiety. Haley reported that she found her trip was much less difficult due to her newfound anchor.

Psychic anchors can be used for everyday worry habits. I try and use them whenever I feel I am worrying unnecessarily about a problem. My anchor brings me back to a more balanced feeling.

PROBLEM SOLVING Okay, so maybe you have got something real to worry about or maybe there is a crisis that just couldn't be averted. It happens. Like you, I have had direct experience with unforeseen obstacles, arguments, explosions, and plain old irritations. There is no spell in the world that can make every day smooth sailing. Life just isn't that simple.

My friend Marian is the president of a large company. She manages more than seven hundred people brilliantly with the help of her shrewd secretary, Kate. Her worst problem, however, was her boss, the CEO, who had less than ten seconds of patience. His secretaries came and went so fast that no one could keep track of their names. Eventually the CEO realized that Kate was a gem and started to insinuate to Marian that they should share Kate. Marian knew that this could not possibly work, since Kate had more than enough to do already. Marian also knew that the minute Kate made a mistake, the CEO would fire her and they'd both lose out. This caused an enormous degree of worry for Marian, who could not find a solution to this politically sticky problem.

Eventually Marian knew that she needed clarity, for her fear and worry had clouded her brain. She cast a spell for clarity to see her way through the problem and found her solution the usual magic way—seemingly by accident.

When Marian went to a meeting in a client's offices, she was kept waiting outside the executive suite. She decided to collect her thoughts and just sit quietly rather than use the time to work or make phone calls. Two secretaries sat near her, talking. Marian overheard the conversation and realized that the secretaries appeared to do different things. She asked them how they were organized and they explained. One was a stenographer trained to be a whiz at typing and filing, while the other was more the outer-world personality who took phone calls and arranged meetings. They worked for the three executives in the main suite. Marian was intrigued by this setup, since she could see how this might help her out. The best part of Kate was her ability to juggle Marian's schedule and manage the constant stream of phone calls. Kate was a fine typist, but that was time-consuming. Eventually, Marian employed this same method and the CEO was placated. Just to be safe, Marian did sit down with the CEO before they started this new routine to clarify that she was in charge of hiring and firing, so that if there was a problem, he would come to her. So far the arrangement is working well.

This situation is not uncommon. Often, someone else's behavior makes it impossible for us to get our jobs done or our goals met. This is definitely frustrating. Solutions are difficult to find when you are in a worried or panicked state. That is why spells for clarity are so useful. Once you regain your objectivity, you can see many more options.

Often problem solving can be approached by using a combination of spells. Clearing spells can remove obstacles or show you obstacles that you don't know are in the way. Staying power can give you the patience to stay with the situation and to allow yourself the time to find a solution. A spell for clarity is often very useful, too, because we get attached to our goal and our "track" to success, and we lose our objectivity, sometimes to the point of using only "tunnel vision." A spell for clarity gives you back a broad view and allows you to see many options you didn't know existed.

GRATITUDE

Since this chapter is about enhancing ongoing enterprises, it is a good time to assess how far you've come since you started your path to success. If you have an ongoing enterprise at this time, it is certainly an excellent time to express gratitude for getting as far as you have.

Gratitude is sort of a psychic insurance policy. By recognizing the blessings of your efforts thus far, you are consciously telling the universe and yourself that you believe in and see the magic you have created. The universe likes getting credit where it is due, as we all do. Since the universe likes to be appreciated, a gratitude spell is a way of saying you are not taking anything for granted.

Doing a gratitude spell is easy, but it is best not to stop there; you can show it to those who have helped you along the way too. It is always life-enhancing to take time to show people appreciation. It makes for better relationships and encourages continued support.

Tithing is another form of gratitude and an excellent way to show thanks when your success involves money or abundance. Tithing is giving away a portion of your profits, goods, or services to those who need them. I happen to believe that tithing is one of the most important gratitude rituals you could ever do and that if we all tithed a little more consciously, we wouldn't have such appalling poverty in our world.

Giving a portion of your assets away is difficult, I know. But it is difficult only when we think that we'll never get it back or that somehow we'll only be poorer for it. It goes back to the fear we were all raised with, that there is "not enough to go around." Practice tithing whatever you feel comfortable with and build from there. Even the tiniest gesture of sharing your bounty and success will be noticed—both by the universe and you. It is enormously powerful to be in a position to give, particularly after you've received.

Giving back is just part of the cycle of receiving. You can't just take all the time. The universe doesn't tolerate too much hoarding or selfishness—that is, when you only consider your own flow of abundance and not how you fit into the world at large. If you do get carried away with your success and possibly forget to give back in some way, you could be in for some unforeseen lessons in the art of giving. The universe just might take what you have and put it somewhere else. Sooner or later, you have to give something back, so it might as well be your choice.

SPELL BASICS

COLOR: Green and yellow
DAY OF THE WEEK: Sunday and Friday
TIME OF DAY: First hour after sunset
TIME OF THE MONTH: Waxing moon
HERBS: Mint, sage, nutmeg

Spell for
CONTINUED GROWTH

On a Sunday when the moon is waxing
and in the first hour of darkness,
light a yellow candle and a green candle.
Place a small plant next to the candles.
In a vessel made of natural fiber, place one
or more of the following:
mint, nutmeg, or sage.

SAY ALOUD:

I offer my voice to the universe
to raise the energy of air.
I offer the elements of fire, earth, and water
to manifest the power of growth.
Newness and renewal,
breath and light,
I affirm that growth is healthy and right.
I turn this over to the universe and say
So be it.
And so it is.

Blow out the candles.
Place a small part of the herbal offering
into the soil.

Spell for
SPACIOUSNESS FOR GROWTH
AND INCREASING POTENTIAL

On a Thursday during a waxing moon
and in the third hour of darkness,
light a purple candle and a green candle.
Place favorite flowers in a vase with water.
Take a green cloth and fold it over four times.

SAY ALOUD:

On this day of Jupiter and expansive energy,
I ask the elements to join me in opening the field,
increasing potential.
With each of the following four phrases,
unfold one part of the cloth:
Fire ignites new possibilities.
Earth opens to new ground.
I breathe air in for spaciousness.
Water nourishes new life.
And as I open to potential so does my success.
I turn this over to the universe with faith.
So be it.
And so it is.

Blow out the candles.
Keep the cloth open until the moon is full.
You may use it for charms in the future.

Spell to

CREATE A POSITIVE PERSONAL ATMOSPHERE

This spell can be done during any day of the week and during any moon cycle.

Light a white candle.
Place a glass of water next to the candle.
Sit quietly before the flame, gazing into it.
Breathe calmly until you are relaxed.
Close your eyes.
Imagine yourself in a serene place.
Breathe in serenity, feel a part of the balance
and tranquillity.
Open your eyes. Breathe with that feeling.
Close your eyes again, this time seeing yourself
in the place where you want
to change your personal atmosphere.
Invoke the feeling of serenity there. Breathe with it.
Stay with it as long as you can.
Open your eyes. Drink some water.

SAY ALOUD:

So be it.
And so it is.

Blow out the candle. Use the water on a plant.
Repeat as often as you like.

Spell to
INCREASE STAYING POWER

On a Tuesday during a waxing moon
and in the first hour of darkness,
light an orange candle.
Place a glass of tea next to the candle.

SAY ALOUD:

*Under the evening of Mars
in this hour of Saturnian commitment,
I raise my voice to the universe.
I ask that a current of patience and endurance
be brought to me with ease and grace.
I affirm my faith in mystery
that my wishes manifest
to their fullest potential.
So be it.
And so it is.*

Take a sip of tea or spill some into a plant.
Allow the candle to burn until you go to sleep.

Spell for
EASE IN MANAGEMENT

On a Friday during the second hour of darkness,
light a pink candle.
Place pink or orange flowers in a vase with water.
Place the peel of a lemon and some lavender
in a vessel made of a natural substance.

SAY ALOUD:

May Venus and the Sun's great power
join together with the natural forces
of the universe in this call for ease.
My own heart
and the light of all those I encounter
manifest in productive, life-enhancing energy.
I open to this potential in its greatest form
and within the laws of the greater good.
So be it.
And so it is.

Blow out the candle.
Place the flowers and the offering in a place
where others are exposed to it.
Dispose of it on the full moon.

Spell for
A PSYCHIC ANCHOR

*This spell can be done during any moon cycle,
during any day of the week. It is best to repeat
this spell once a week for four consecutive weeks.*

Light a green candle.
Place a glass of water next to the candle.
Place some dried thyme in a fireproof vessel.
Sit before the flame of the candle.
Close your eyes.
Breathe in and out until you feel relaxed.
Visualize a place where you feel peaceful.
Breathe the peace in.
Stay with that feeling as long as you can.
When you feel ready, create a gesture
that you can do easily
(i.e., bring your hands together, touch your
forehead, raise your hand, wiggle your finger).
Use this gesture several times while you are in your
state of peacefulness.

SAY ALOUD:

*I call upon my peace with this gesture.
So be it.
And so it is.*

Burn the thyme, allowing it to smolder.
Blow out the candle and throw away the ash.

Spell for
CLARITY

On a Wednesday during a waxing moon
and in the first hour of darkness,
light a blue candle and place it
next to a glass of water.
Place some celery and lavender before the candle.

SAY ALOUD:

With the concepts of Mercury
and the healing power of the Sun,
I ask that the guardians
light my way to clarity.
I open my eyes and my heart
to a path that leads to success
within the greater good.
I relinquish my control over "how"
and allow the universe to create the way.
I affirm my faith in this process.
So be it.
And so it is.

Drink some water and place four drops
on the candle, then blow the candle out.
Dispose of the offering on the full moon.

Spell for
GRATITUDE

On a Friday or Sunday during a waxing moon,
light a candle in your favorite color.
Place your favorite flowers in a vase of water
next to the candle.
Put some money in front of the candle.

SAY ALOUD:

I offer my gratitude to the guardians
for making my success possible.
I offer my continued faith to the universe
and its infinite abundance.
I give thanks to be in this life
and to know the power of manifestation.
My gratitude is expressed to all:
those known, unknown, and myself.
I turn these words of thanks over to the universe
with love and say
So be it.
And so it is.

Allow your candle to burn as long as you like.
Give the money away to a cause
or to someone in need.

FIVE

Spells to Get Through Inactivity, Reversals, and Lean Times

Spell Basics

*Spell for Spaciousness
and Tolerance*

Spell for Purifying Emotions

Spell for Handing Over Despair

Spell for Protection

Charm to Hold Prosperity Steady

Spell to Enjoy Fallow Times

As discussed earlier in the book, everyone has natural cycles of energy. There is a spring, summer, fall, and winter period for us all, and this affects our projects and our path to success. Everything has a beginning and a middle, and everything has an end, too, as much as we all hate to admit it. It is that ending, or winter part, that now needs to be addressed. Even in a long-term ongoing enterprise, when you know that an ending is improbable, there will be times that are leaner, inactive, or simply less productive.

This part of the natural cycle is by far hardest for all of us to deal with. Even if you are essentially lazy or at ease with doing nothing, this is the kind of nothing that can be very uncomfortable—because it is out of our control.

If you take a step back and look at how we live, you'll see what I mean. We are accustomed to controlling things that cause us discomfort. If it is too hot out, we put on air-conditioning. If it is cold, we use heat. Got a headache? Take some aspirin. We are so used to problem solving that when something is out of our hands, most of us don't know how to deal with it.

We are simply not taught how to go through fallow times or times when it is best to do nothing rather than push. But fallow times come anyway. When you start working with them, they can become as gratifying as those big bursts of initiating energy. When you push against them, however, you can exhaust yourself and still have no tangible results.

I am very familiar with the area and have been working consciously with it for some time. I find it is practically against my nature to "not do" anything. Don't think that you're the only one who gets afraid or frustrated when things slow down.

I am used to working all year round like I used to in the corporate world. In my new career as a consultant and writer, I have much more power over my own schedule and much more obvious cycles. After I finish writing a book, I experience a natural fallow period. It is much needed for intellectual and creative recovery, yet I still get nervous that I am not using my time to create something else.

The fallow or inactive time can be filled with what I call existential angst. This is a feeling of foreboding mixed with guilt and worry, which is highly unpleasant, completely unproductive, and entirely unnecessary. Yet it still happens to most people I know.

Working with fallow energy may seem like a paradox—how do you "work" in a time of inactivity? This kind of working is an inner experience, not an energy of outer manifestation. It is learning to let things be, to tolerate stillness, to use inactivity as a way of regenerating. I know, though, that this is easier said than done. That is why spells can be so effective. In situations of "nothingness," magic has a greater potential to show up.

THE EMOTION RESPONSE

FEAR What I call existential angst incorporates a number of darker emotions. This is a complex situation. We react differently when we think things are out of control, going bad, or reversing. Dealing with fear is not so easy. Since we all seem to be averse to unpleasant emotions, there is a lot of denial going around. First, you have to admit that you feel fear. Since we are also encouraged to "never let them see you sweat," fear isn't so socially acceptable. That is often a reason why we don't allow ourselves to feel it.

My client Emily, an importer of Eastern European art, was experiencing an enormous downswing in her business. She came to me for help, looking for a spell for recovery. She told me that she was really angry at the turn of events that brought her business down, all of which were out of her control. Government tariffs had been prohibitive, several of her suppliers had folded, and as a result, she had missed the whole buying season. Emily had the idea that her spell could magically fix things and that she could still make the most of this year's sales. Now, magic works very well when you are working with potential, but by Emily's description of events, there didn't seem to be a whole lot to work with. My assessment was most dispiriting for Emily, and her anger melted quickly into fear. How was she going to get through this if things didn't work out her way? How was she going to keep her business going, make money, and continue to live? Her fear took her straight into survival issues, as if the situation was going to be the end of her life. Of course, it wasn't, and we immediately worked with dissipating her fear so that she could see her way through this time.

Emily's anger was her defense mechanism, but it was also dangerous denial. If you try to change the outer world when it simply cannot be moved, you waste a lot of energy and risk making things worse. For instance, if Emily had proceeded with a spell to renew her business, she might have carried on as if the market were going to right itself, when clearly the time had passed for that opportunity. This could have been costly and much more financially damaging than facing the situation and working with it realistically.

Emily did work with her fallow period. She cast a spell for spaciousness and tolerance so that she could open herself up to ways of getting though this tough time. She decided to downsize her business temporarily and look for other ways to make money. She had so much experience with the Eastern European market system, she found that she could market herself as a consultant for other importers. Her consulting revenues compensated her adequately—she didn't end up homeless—and now, in her recovery stage, she keeps both businesses going. Emily's importing reversal proved to be more than just a fallow period; it was an opportunity to reassess and eventually expand her business.

COPING WITH FAILURE Since we are a culture driven toward success, there is a great deal of fear in failure. This is one reason why so many people don't even try to achieve their goals. Their fear of failure is so overwhelming that they can't take any chances. Frank Loesser's lyric in *How to Succeed in Business Without Really Trying* says it all: "Year after year after fiscal . . . never-take-a-risk all year."

Even if you are a "company guy" or a conformist, even if you don't like to shake things up, you will still find times in your life when you have to face failure. Recent years have been filled with layoffs from even the most stable and seemingly safe companies. Financial markets have gone up and down, and what used to be the American way of playing the game and getting ahead just doesn't work so well anymore. We can't count on any system staying in place; our world is shifting and changing every day and forcing us to be more creative as a result.

Being prepared and working with the changes around you will be discussed more thoroughly in Chapter Seven. For now, we need to focus on the immediate issue of failure, whether it is within your control or not.

The best way to cope with failure is to immediately identify it as a rerouting of your passage to success. Julie Andrews as Maria von Trapp in *The Sound of Music* said, "Whenever God closes a door, somewhere he's opened a window." This may seem a bit too optimistic for you, but that's really the only way to give yourself immediate perspective. Failing at one thing doesn't mean your life is over; it means that the route you were on was not the best one—it's time to backtrack and renavigate.

I remember failing my driving test the first time I took it. I thought my life would end; I had to wait a whole six weeks until I could take it again. I passed it the second time. So what? How could that possibly have been a rerouting of opportunity? I don't know, but I shudder to think that if I had gotten my license at the wrong time, I might not be here to tell about it. You have to trust the universe to know what is right for you and when.

Fallow times also occur before you shift into a new life. Particularly if you are going to make a big change, like a career or lifestyle change, you may experience a time of emptiness. This allows you to adjust to the coming change. Whenever you release part of what you consider to be your old life—and even if you can't wait to get rid of it—you may experience a little fear and sadness as a reaction. After all, it is what you have known, and even if you want to change it, it is letting go of a part of you.

SADNESS: A NATURAL REACTION Not often a word associated with a path to success, sadness is a very real part of the cycle. When we go through loss in any sense, sadness is a part of the healing process. If you are particularly attached to your goal, you may feel sad that it is not happening or even that it is over. Endings are not easy in many cases, and they are especially disagreeable when you feel as if you had no control over them. Failure is a judgment that you may make about your ability to reach your goal, but take care not to make it a judgment about yourself.

Grief, the mourning process, is absolutely natural, not that we like it. If you find yourself going through lean or fallow times and you feel sadness, it is quite normal. Think of winter, a naturally fallow time, and how the barren trees and landscape can evoke a feeling of sadness, even desolation. The worst thing you can do is resist the feelings you have. This is easy to do because we like to fix things so much—remember, take that aspirin if you have a headache. It really is best not to try to medicate your emotions unless they immobilize you. If you are simply feeling loss, sadness, or grief and you understand the source of it (i.e., your business folded, you didn't get the contract you wanted, your goal has come and gone), allow yourself to feel the pain. It won't stay any longer than necessary and it will purge you of anything that could prevent you from moving on. If you don't allow the grief, it will stay inside you until you do feel it.

Sadness denied can become an overwhelming burden that creates a load of energy you continue to carry around with you. You've probably heard the term "baggage" used to describe relationship issues that haven't been worked through. This term is equally applicable to goal-oriented projects. If you don't work out the emotional responses to failure, you will take them with you into your next goal.

Tom, an investment banker, was laid off from his very high-paying job at a well-known corporation. His dismissal wasn't particularly personal; the company needed to cut back and he didn't make the cut. Since Tom had a decent track record, he felt that he could find employment fairly easily. He used his "stiff upper lip" to get through the process of outplacement and to finally land a new job. During the fallow time when Tom was not working, he kept busy and didn't allow himself to feel any "negative" emotions. After all, he reasoned, you have to keep up a good attitude in order to get another job.

After Tom started in his new job, he relaxed into a less frenetic flow. He felt that he had overcome the layoff rather well and was back on his feet. However, he was having a hard time getting excited about his new company and he was expressing lackluster energy in his work. He came to me for a spell for reigniting his drive. In our discussion, he complained that this company wasn't like the last one; the people, the location, even the decor was not as good as his last place of employment. Tom simply didn't want to be happy in this new job. I began to question him as to why he had bothered to take the job and then noticed that he looked rather sad when he looked back into the past. Tom never allowed himself to feel the sadness of leaving his company, of being asked to leave, even though it wasn't personal, and he never coped with his feelings of failure around it.

I gave Tom a spell for purifying his emotional self so that his feelings of sadness could be felt and then dissipate. He is a dutiful type, so Tom did the spell and called me to say that he had spent a solitary, moody weekend at home but was feeling better later in the week. He hasn't been back for any more spells but has kept in touch. He is back in the swing of his business.

Since Tom allowed his pain to emerge, he didn't keep it buried in his unconscious. If he had, he could have stayed very discontented and eventually jeopardized his new job. No matter how hard any of us try to dismiss sadness, it will sit inside you stubbornly until you deal with it. It may be unpleasant for a time, but allowing the healing process makes your chances for success that much greater.

DESPAIR: THE DARK SIDE OF SADNESS Pain and grief, however, can sometimes be overwhelming. This is when you must consider ways of finding your way back to the light. You may fall into a harsher place, where the judgment of failure falls onto yourself. This is despair.

My close friend Raye had a constant fight with an eating disorder. She was courageous enough to face it and took the practical approaches for healing—therapy and doctor's help. She gradually found the sources of her problem and worked with them until she felt as if she had gained ground. It seemed as if she had finally licked the problem. Then, without warning or obvious cause, she once again fell into her self-destructive behavior. This was most upsetting for all her friends, because there was so much fear that she might not make it. For Raye, her seeming failure threw her into despair that sapped her of her basic will to live. She had done all that was known to and available for a cure, but still she fell back. She had tried so hard, had been so courageous, that it was too difficult, from her vantage point, to imagine going through therapy again; her view was "it hasn't worked, why bother?" She was ready to throw in the towel. Raye exhibited dangerous signs of depression.

I don't want to give you the idea that spell casting is a panacea for depression or any other difficult passages. What I do want to communicate is that performing spells is a way of opening up hope and the possibility that magic, the universe, the higher power, can come through when you just don't know how to cope.

Raye indulged me by casting a spell simply to hand over her despair to the universe so that she could breathe and see some light. She was a most skeptical and difficult subject, but she did it and that was all that counted. Eventually, Raye sought help once more, and she cannot put her finger on what brought about her turning point. There was no moment of epiphany. Frankly, I don't know what happened either, but she did make it through and is healthy again; she has not lapsed back into her destructive behavior. Somewhere she found the energy to keep going.

Despair, like fear, is paralyzing. It can give you the impression that there is no way out. Although spell casting is a useful tool to ease the feeling of oppression, I must recommend that you use it in conjunction with professional help. Despair, in its darkest form, can lead to suicide—through eating disorders, drug addiction, or consciously taking or destroying your own life.

USING YOUR FALLOW TIME

So far, this discussion of fallow times has been less than agreeable. Fear, sadness, despair . . . who needs it? Not all fallow times are so unpleasant and dramatic. They can be productive in a different way, but you have to recognize them for what they are and use them wisely.

ALLOWING There's that word again, *allowing*. Sometimes it feels like an enemy, especially when you want control. Allowing is the opposite of control. You just have to wait it out. When you realize that you are in a fallow or lean time, you can allow yourself to lean into it.

I finally got used to the fallow cycles in my life, and now I go on great vacations, using the time to replenish my energy and enjoy life from a different, nonaggressive perspective. Even when money is tight, it is a good time to go away, leave your structured life for a while, and look around the world a bit. Use frequent flier miles, stay with your aunt and uncle, or trade the use of your house for someone else's in a different place. Get creative in the way you explore, relax, and renew.

If you go to Florida in the winter, nature's fallow season, you are bound to see many vacationing farmers. They know their fields are lying fallow and they work very hard most of the year to grow crops. The winter is the only time they can really kick back. They give us an excellent example of how to use a fallow time for pleasure.

WHAT TO DO WITH YOU: THE ART OF HUNKERING DOWN Fallow times are internal. Your energy is not in the right place to go out into the world and make things happen. It is a great time to look at your life, your goals, your home, your relationships, whatever you tend to ignore when you are in the full swing of creating success.

It's a great time to clean out closets, go through old documents, take a class, explore life beyond goal-oriented tasks.

This is a hard lesson for most of us to learn. Don't kid yourself that it's easy to lean into a fallow time and use it wisely. Especially if you work in a job that demands that you be there fifty weeks a year, you aren't going to find it easy to say, "Sorry, just off to the mountains for a few months—it's my fallow time." The challenge in this situation is to find a way to give yourself what you need, when you need it, even when life demands you keep producing.

My friend Keith was going through a mild fallow period. His job gave him great pleasure, but the company was going through lean times and he hadn't received a raise in two years. He had to repay student loans and debt so that his disposable income was fairly limited. It was a quiet time in his life, no big social occasions and nothing really exciting going on. He was sort of bored and mildly worried about money.

Although he's a skeptic, he is a close friend of mine, which means that he'll try out a spell or two. First, he made a charm to hold prosperity steady, so that he wouldn't have to deal with unforeseen debt or disaster. Then he did a spell for protection, again with the idea of keeping himself in a steady state and not getting into dangerous or unnecessarily draining situations. Finally, Keith did a spell for enjoying fallow times. I am glad to say that all his spells worked, since it would have been very tiresome for me if they hadn't.

For about a three-month period, Keith's lifestyle shifted subtly. He read more and spent more time outdoors, biking, hiking, and walking around town. He also wanted to take a cooking class but didn't want to spend the money. He found that he could assist the chef and take the classes he wanted to for free. This ended up being an exceptionally fun pastime and he met a woman in the class whom he began to date. He even found dating was a pleasure on a budget. He was able to cook dinner, take her to art galleries, and carry on with his outdoorsy things without looking cheap. Since everyone goes through fallow times, he wasn't ashamed to admit that money was a little tight and his date seemed to understand.

Keith, now in a completely different, much more high-powered position in his company, looks back on those fallow times with some nostalgia. His life was much simpler then and even more creative. Now he is ruled by cellular phones, fax machines, and round-the-clock meetings.

Fallow times do not last forever and they can offer you a time in your life that has a quality of simplicity hard to maintain in the world's usual tempo of progress and growth.

As we saw with Keith, there are ways to make fallow times enjoyable. This is possible only when you remove negativity from your mind and heart. For Keith, this meant doing things that afforded him some enjoyment without evoking fear.

To get to that state, you need perspective. Since fallow times do not last forever, you need to recognize that everything changes, even the flow of success. The fallow state is a natural one and is always followed by rebirth, like spring, growth, as in summer, and winter yet again.

RELEASING NEGATIVITY Living in our society, one in which fallow times are often seen as "bad" times, makes it difficult to keep that perspective. Using the turn of the seasons helps us to see that stillness and "death" are part of a natural cycle, but even with that rational understanding, it may be hard to enjoy it.

A good way of looking at a fallow period is as a time to enjoy the quiet and stillness of hibernating. Instead of looking to the outside world for recognition and action, look in your own cave, so to speak. Most of us have an enormous amount of stuff we've acquired in our lives. A fallow time is a good time to enjoy it.

One past summer, my sister was going through a very quiet time; her consulting work was slowing down as it often did during vacation season. She was not really in the mood to go out and socialize, yet she didn't want to just sit in front of the TV—nor was she into reading since the fine weather made her want to be active. She was uncomfortable in her own fallow season and tried to ignore it by going after new business. Since it just wasn't a time for her business to be busy, she didn't get anywhere. She was actually falling into a state of negativity in which she couldn't find anything useful to do with herself; she became grumpy.

In an effort to relieve this state of malaise, she cast a spell to release negativity, and when the moon shifted, she cast her spell for enjoying her fallow time. Her spell allowed her to open up to the opportunity around her and she found herself exploring the stuff she had been storing in a shed behind her house. Among the many forgotten possessions, she found an old grill, her old bicycle, a lot of gardening tools, and some old tables she'd picked up at garage sales. She quickly became absorbed in rehabilitating the grill, the bicycle, and the tables. In her spare moments, she tended her garden more assiduously and was pleased at the variety of blooms it produced. Even when her work became more active again, she didn't stop enjoying her bike, the grill, and her garden. She seemed to appreciate the time alone and the self-created tasks with no goal hanging in the wings.

This brings to mind that old idea of a hobby. While the word *hobby* makes me flinch, bringing to mind the musty old stamp and coin collection I was supposed to have kept as a child, I now understand its real meaning. A hobby is not a task; it is an interest. Many of us seem to have lost respect for putting time into things that bring us pleasure for pleasure's sake. The art of living is not just to get through or get by; it is to enjoy and create what there is around you.

You may find this information especially irritating if you are in a typically stretched family situation—working couples with kids. You may already feel that you don't have enough time even to have a fallow period, let alone enjoy one. If you have to manage a family and a career, it may be impossible for you to allow yourself to sink into stillness at times. It happens. When the demands of the world are so great and so immediate—your children, your mortgage—it may be necessary for you to give up your own needs temporarily. The danger here is giving over completely, never returning to your own rhythm, even when you can create the time to do so again. When the demands of your world are stretching you to your limit, it is you who need the fallow time most of all. Look for ways to give yourself a little time, maybe a few hours a week, to let yourself rest. Even small increments sprinkled through a week can help you maintain more personal energy.

I have many friends and clients who are clever in the way they find time for themselves. Baby-sitting co-ops help, rotating responsibility for children so that you have a few evenings or weekends off. Giving your partner time off, even weekends off to be alone, helps. I even know people who turn down promotions and job situations that would challenge their ability to have time to themselves. Instead of a job that required a lot of travel, a client of mine opted for a job that kept him close to home. Some would rather have less cash and more life; this choice is being made more and more often.

THE IMPORTANCE OF BEING FALLOW Fallow times afford us the opportunity to know what is going on in our own heads and hearts. If you're always on the go, taking care of others, and squeaking in time for sleep or leisure in the odd spare moment, you are in danger of a severe midlife crisis. This may seem a harsh threat, but allow me to explain. A midlife crisis is when you wake up one day and you wonder what you've done with your life, who you are, where you are going, and why you aren't further along now that you are thirty-five, forty, forty-five, fifty, fifty-five, sixty. You can be any age in your life and experience that crisis. Fallow times are periods all through your life that are there for you to use—to assess what gives you pleasure, what interests you, what is really important in your life, and what is superfluous. You can take time to discard things that are no longer useful; you may find that things that gave you pleasure in your youth wear thin as your life goes on. You may also find that, as you grow older, different things in life hold interest and you feel freer to explore.

If you don't take time to listen to yourself and allow your needs to be felt, you are giving away the power to live your life to the fullest and hence the ability to feel successful.

Being able to be still, quiet, and alone may seem like a luxury you can't afford, but I'm here to tell you that you can't afford not to.

FINISHING A FALLOW TIME Just when you surrender, sinking into cozy life in your cave, the world is going to turn again. After adjusting to the quiet rhythm of your own needs and interests, you will find yourself being drawn back to the outer world. As you leave the fallow time, you bring with you new power.

Look at what can be learned in the "winter" part of abundance. You can move through pain, fear, and anger so that you won't carry it with you in your life. You can reconnect to things that make you happy: sewing, reading, cooking, tinkering, whatever pastime or hobby that adds to your pleasure in life. You may discover new passions that could contribute to success in the future. You never know. In fact, you really never know, for the true gifts of the fallow time are not known until the following harvest.

If you work with your fallow time and allow it to take its course, you are going to benefit by living with less fear. Those who understand the art of stillness and how to use a fallow time are less afraid of it happening again. Less fear breeds more power, and more power ultimately leads to more success.

SPELL BASICS

Spells to go through fallow times are a little diverse for simplifying into straight spell basics, but you can use these general guidelines.

COLORS: Green for money
White for purification
Purple for spaciousness
FLOWERS: White (carnations)
HERBS: Eucalyptus and lavender

For Releasing Spells

DAY OF THE WEEK: Any
TIME OF THE MONTH: Waning moon

For Increasing Spells

DAY OF THE WEEK: Thursday
TIME OF THE MONTH: Waxing moon

Spell for
SPACIOUSNESS AND TOLERANCE

On a Thursday during a waxing moon,
light a green candle and a white candle.
Place eucalyptus oil on your heart center.
Place white flowers in a vase with water.

SAY ALOUD:

*In the flow of the spacious evening sky
I breathe in the air of light and openness.
I ask that the elements join with me in creating space
in my heart, in my mind, and in my life.
I affirm I am guided through this cycle
with my trust and faith.*

Breathe in, filling your lungs up,
then slowly release your breath.

SAY ALOUD:

*I am spacious and tolerant.
And so it is done.*

Blow out the candles.
Use eucalyptus oil on your heart center
whenever you feel overwhelmed.

Spell for
PURIFYING EMOTIONS

*This spell may be performed on any evening
during a waning moon.*

Place these elements in front of you:
a white candle,
a bowl of water,
a bowl of salt,
dried sage in a vessel in which it can be burned.

SAY ALOUD:

*I gather these elements to cleanse any toxicity that
may cloud my ability to be in the flow of this cycle.
I release negativity in my fire*
(wave your hand over or through the flame)
I release blockages in my earth
(rub salt on your hands)
I clear my own air
(wave the smoldering sage in front of you)
and I purify my water
(dip your hands in water).
*I ask that this release be gentle.
I affirm my trust and faith in my own abundant flow.
So be it.
And so it is.*

Dispose of the ingredients immediately.
Use the candle again for any other
waning moon spell.

Spell for
HANDING OVER DESPAIR

This spell can be done any evening
during a waning moon.
During a waxing moon, use the
Spell for Spaciousness and Tolerance.

Light a white candle.
Place white flowers in a vase with water.

SAY ALOUD:

In my rage, despair, and darkness,
I call upon the guardians, my guides,
God and Goddess.
Take this burden
from my heart, body,
mind, and spirit.
I release this pain freely and willingly.
I ask to be guided back to the light
and that this be done immediately
for the greater good and for the good of myself.
So be it.
And so it is.

Let the candle burn as long as you wish.
When the flowers are dead, throw them away
outside your home.

Spell for
PROTECTION

On a Sunday during a waxing moon
and in the third hour of darkness,
light an orange candle.
Place carnations in a vase with water.
Place some basil in a natural vessel
in front of the flame.

SAY ALOUD:

I call in the guardians and the power
of the masculine and feminine.
I surround myself with the fire of protection.
The earth's grace supports me.
The winds bring me gentle shifts,
and the flow of water eases the energy of this time.
I affirm I believe in this protection
and I release my fears
so that I may connect
to the pulse of life.
I ask that this be done within the greater good.
So be it.
And so it is.

Let the candle burn as long as you like.
Use the basil in your charm to hold prosperity
steady or throw it out on the full moon.

Charm to
HOLD PROSPERITY STEADY

On a Friday during a waxing moon
and in the second hour of darkness,
light a green candle.
Take a green piece of cloth and cut it into
a diamond shape.
In the center of the fabric,
place a silver dime inside a white carnation.
Also place some nuts in their casings,
basil, and some dried lavender.
Allow four drops of water to fall onto the carnation.
Gather up the ends of the cloth
and sew them together with orange thread.
Make four knots with the thread before cutting it.

SAY ALOUD:

I charge this charm with the power of protection,
that it holds my prosperity steady
so that I may live with ease
during this time of sparsity.
I claim this power as my own for the greater good.
So be it.
And so it is.

Blow out the candle.
Carry it with you and put it in a place
you regularly see.

Spell to
ENJOY FALLOW TIMES

On a Friday during a waxing moon
and in the second hour of darkness,
light a candle of your favorite color.
Place yellow or pink flowers in a vase with water.
Place some lavender in a natural vessel
next to the flowers.

SAY ALOUD:

*I open to the easy vibration
of God and Goddess,
to the time of quiet and repose.
I ask the guardians to guide me through this time
so that I may emerge with inner wisdom.
I participate in this natural shift in energy
and I bless the gifts it bears.
I trust that I am in the flow of infinite abundance.
So be it.
And so it is.*

Blow out the candle. Repeat this spell any day,
regardless of the moon phase,
after the first time it is performed.
Dispose of the lavender on the full moon.

Spells for Recovery and Expansion

Spell Basics

Spell for Recovery

*Spell to Increase
Business Opportunities*

Spell to Expand Space

Power Bundles

Spell to Attract New Investors

Spell for Diversification

Spell for Acquisition

Some think that this chapter should go straight to the president's economic advisors, since our economy is always searching for expansion and recovery. However, instead of taking on a large system I don't thoroughly understand, I think it is more productive to start with the individual: you and me, since we eventually make up Them. The economic cycle of our country is a reflection of the whole, of what each of us contributes. If we all start to work with our own cycles, the whole economic cycle would hold less fear and therefore be more easily dealt with.

This chapter deals with two issues: first, recovery after a lean and fallow period, and second, the idea of expanding beyond what you have at hand. Recovery is like a rebirth and expansion is a robust expression of energy that brings a little fun back into your path to success.

RECOVERY

Perhaps *resurrection* would be a better word for this phase of your cycle. Certainly, after a difficult fallow period, you may feel as if you are being reborn, rising from the ashes. This can be a wonderful experience, full of vitality and freedom, hope and eagerness.

Recovery begins during the last phase of a fallow time. Like the first crocus in the melting snow, recovery starts with a glimpse of promise, color, and activity in the outer world.

My client Christiana is an insurance agent who went through a dramatic personal recession. People who had bought policies let them lapse, and even though she had a constant list of prospects, she just didn't make up for her lost income. She adjusted her standard of living accordingly and went into debt just to survive. She bravely worked through the fears surrounding this downward economic spiral and even invested in courses to train her in financial advising. This served her in two ways: to help her understand her own financial state and to potentially add to her business skills so that her income wouldn't rely so much on her policy sales. Finally, after over a year of challenges and keeping the wolf from the door, she came to me for a spell for recovery. She had completed her course and was ready to shift out of her internal time and go aggressively back into the world. I had to question her first to make sure she was ready to make this move. If she was not ready, a spell for recovery would probably not work and could cause her to waste precious energy.

Christiana was almost a different person when we met. She had a new sparkle in her eye and more charisma. Her recessionary atmosphere had lifted. The fact was, she enjoyed the financial advising side more than she had her insurance business. She told me that she had been confiding in a friend how much she enjoyed the course and how it helped her understand financial management more clearly. Quite out of the blue, her friend turned into her first client—just like that. Christiana said that she hadn't even been trying to sell herself but that her friend just stepped into the opportunity. That was the first glimmer of rebirth for Christiana. She hadn't been looking for it, but when she least expected it, a little ray of light came through the clouds.

After performing her spell for recovery, Christiana moved confidently out into the world of financial advising. She felt secure in offering these new services since she believed in herself and had some reassurance from the outside. The insurance business is very compatible with financial planning, so Christiana simply expanded her business potential. Now she has a tidy business going. She still handles insurance, but her real love is her new area.

She looks back into her fallow period and is grateful that it has passed, but she also knows that it brought her unforeseen opportunity.

WHEN TO PERFORM A SPELL FOR RECOVERY Spells for recovery are best performed after you've had your first glimpse of the light—that is, when you are able to find your energy and hopefulness again. This is not to say that your fallow time has to be dramatic, but you'll know the difference between a quiet, internal time versus the beckoning of the outside world.

You can ask yourself if you are ready:

- Are you seeing more potential in the outside world for realizing your goals, dreams, and hopes?
- Are you feeling more social?
- Do you have more energy?
- Are you feeling more at ease in the process of your fallow time?

The universe seems to have its little joke that way. Once you get used to the quieter life and more internal energy, potential knocks on your door and it is time to go out again.

Don't kid yourself, though. If you are still in the throes of your internal time, trying to go back out and fight will be at best exhausting and at worst defeating. Don't go until you are ready and able. Willing just isn't enough.

ONE MORE WORD ON RECOVERY Go slowly. Just because you feel like a million bucks and your energy is returning to its more exuberant level, don't push too hard too quickly.

You can liken it to physical therapy. For instance, if you've broken your leg and it's just out of the cast, you aren't going to run right away. You have to build up the muscle and reacquaint your leg to the weight of your body standing and walking.

If you are coming out of a fallow time, you are also in a healing place, only it is not so obviously physical. Move slowly back into the world and see what may have shifted on the outside while you were exploring your inside. If you jump too quickly into the fray, you may not have as much perspective and hence not as much opportunity. Take your time. Relish the process of rebirth—you have a lot ahead of you.

ENERGY FOR EXPANSION

This is an area somewhat related to recovery. Although expansion is not necessarily derived from a fallow time, it is similar to the process of rebirth. Expansion implies adding energy and potential to that which already exists and thereby increasing the outcome.

You may find that your ongoing enterprise is doing just fine, but you want to grow more or move into something else. Christiana's recovery from her fallow time incorporated some of the energy of expansion; her business became bigger as a result of its own contraction.

When you want to expand in any way, you need to gather in energy, assess or take inventory of your resources, and decide in which direction to expand.

BEWARE OF BANDWAGONS Just because someone else has expanded their enterprise in a certain way, don't be drawn into the idea, too, without careful consideration. My friend Jonathan lost a lot of weight, as did his friend Nick. Nick went on to train for marathons, expanding his enjoyment of his newfound fitness. Jonathan thought he would go for it, too, but he has only a bad back and shin splints to show for it, and his weight is slowly increasing as a result of his inactivity.

Companies are constantly hopping on bandwagons. This age of technology has a lot of wagons to hop onto. There are more and more products—improvements in faxes, computers, telephones, virtual reality, voice-activated response mechanisms . . . it goes on. But where is the market? Just how many of us can afford these things, let alone understand them? A great majority of us just learned how to program our VCRs. Companies may hop on the technological bandwagon and end up on the road to a very small market.

Look around before you expand. See what you are good at, what you enjoy, and consider where you may like to play with success next. It doesn't have to be an offshoot of your enterprise. It can be a complementary business or even a sideline. One interesting hybrid store in New York City is a very good independent video store with a place in the back that sells candles, herbs, crystals, and New Age books. Most people would not think that videos and metaphysical materials were a complementary business, but for the owners of this store, it works.

Expand in ways that make you happy, not just where the market is supposedly going or where the latest fad is. You are much more likely to be happy when you expand in a direction that feeds your individual creativity.

IF YOU HAVE GOT THE ITCH, SCRATCH CARE-FULLY Sometimes the itch to expand starts before you are prepared to scratch it. Particularly for larger-scale ventures, you may have the vision clear in your mind before you even begin to look for financing, partners, or inventory, whatever it is that you'll need to make your vision a reality.

The energy of expansion can be like being tickled. It can be a pleasant, happy sensation and can make you beg for more. It can also be too much of a good thing. Expansion is loaded with seduction for us. We think bigger is better; progress is the best path. We'll go in for expanding a lot more willingly than into a contracting or fallow time. Expansion is an outer, energetic experience. Just because it works with the outside world, however, does not mean it will add to your abundance. Too much expansive energy too quickly leads to explosion.

Your patience skills can be tested during times of expansion. You have to know when to hold back, when to pull back, even, in order to take on the best position. Sometimes this isn't clear. I personally resort to an elemental checklist to see if I'm really ready to go ahead.

If you consider each of the elements and the qualities they represent, you can use it as a way of assessing how prepared you are to expand:

1. FIRE (Passion, creativity, will)

Do you feel inspired to expand into new territory or are you doing it because it seems to be the thing to do? Do you feel connected to your goal? Do you care? Are you willing to commit to more work?

2. EARTH (Money, health, physical things)

Do you have the resources you need to expand or do you need to acquire them? Do you feel comfortable taking on debt if needed? Are you physically capable of handling this new area? Would this adversely affect your health?

3. AIR (Ideas, mental state, contracts)

Do you believe in this new venture? Do you harbor any doubts that this is a good idea? Do you understand the implications of going into this process? Are there rules or regulations you need to be familiar with? Are there others who understand your reasoning and support you in this interest?

4. WATER (Emotions, relationships)

How do you feel about expansion? Does it evoke fear, excitement? Are you worrying excessively about this possibility? Is your heart in this? Do you feel comfortable with the people who are involved with your expansion? Do you trust them?

If you can get through this checklist and feel reasonably sure that you're ready to move ahead, read on. If you feel that perhaps there are one or two areas you are not quite comfortable with, you may find it more useful to refer back to Chapter Three and perform the Spell to Clear the Elements. Then you can see what comes up and if it is possible to continue with your idea to expand.

PLAYFULNESS The desire to expand does not arise out of need or lack. It is unlikely that you are expanding a venture while you are in trouble or being threatened. If you are expanding under those circumstances, you may want to rethink it. The whole notion of expanding is building more onto a foundation that is solidly in place. If your foundation isn't solid, too much pressure on it can collapse the whole thing. You've heard of the straw that broke the camel's back.

Expansion is like creating a goal that augments and continues your original path to success. Your desire to grow bigger is a self-directed process. This means you can play around with it and you don't have to put the pressure of a deadline on yourself, at least not in the beginning.

Because expansion energy has the power to include so much potential, you may want to play with it before committing to a plan. The energy of expansion acts like a fisherman's net. It is cast out far and wide, and when gathered back into the boat, it may be filled with lots of beautiful fish, some poisonous fish, and maybe a few old rubber tires. Expansive energy opens you up to a great deal—but not everything you haul in may be appropriate.

A playful attitude and patience can help here. If you aren't in a hurry to jump on the first good-looking fish in your net, you may find a treasure farther on.

INCREASING BUSINESS OPPORTUNITIES Sybil, the owner of a small home landscaping service, had been reaping decent profits for the last five years. She had a good team of people working for her and her business was well established in her community. Sybil got the itch to expand. Since she had good credit and continuing profits, she knew that she would be able to get a loan from her bank if she wanted to. She also had plenty of help; the local college always provided her with enough part-timers to carry extra work if it was needed. The community supported her business and, in turn, she gave back by donating money and services for charity auctions. In short, Sybil had a pretty model business going.

Those of you going through hard times or feeling risk averse may sit back and say, "Don't do it! Why risk what you've got?" Sybil wouldn't have responded well to that. She had the itch and she wanted to scratch it.

Unfortunately, Sybil had no idea what to do in order to expand. She didn't really want to expand the landscaping end of her business. Her itch demanded that she try her hand at something else. But what?

She came to me for a spell for finding out what she should do. We started by casting a spell to increase business opportunities. I asked her to wait a moon cycle (a month) to see what came up. Sybil resisted waiting since she really wanted to have a project started. She decided to carry a notebook around with her for a month and write down everything that she came across that interested her. By the time we met next, she had many pages of things written—some realistic and others far-fetched. For instance, she thought there was a need for a farm and garden equipment repair center, but she didn't have the interest in doing that. She looked around nearby towns and talked to some of her suppliers, but she didn't find anything inspiring. In fact, she was slightly put out when she learned that a big corporate center was going to be built a few miles away from her business that would no doubt be landscaped by the architect and meant less land for homes.

This is where Sybil's spell kicked in. Some days after our meeting she was at the town hall paying her property tax when she overheard people talking about the restaurants and neighborhoods nearby. Sybil was clever, if a bit impolite, to eavesdrop, and she heard that these were the people representing the development at the new corporate center. She asked if she could help them, and it turned out they were looking for a place to have lunch. With her community spirit flying high, Sybil gave them a number of options and told them how the town was full of small business owners. She gave them her card in case she could be of any further service.

She got a call the following day from one of the people asking if she knew a good indoor landscape service. The new center needed to contract with a local business to take care of the design and maintenance of its indoor plants and shrubs. Sybil used her itch to expand to give her the nerve to say, at that point, that she could do it.

While she did have to scramble a bit to seem experienced, she did provide a reasonable estimate and was eventually hired. The bank gave her the loan she needed. She used her local part-time college help to staff this business, since it required more manpower but less expertise. She was on her way.

It is interesting to note that Sybil's spell worked here very much for the greater good; that is, everyone benefited; no one suffered. At first she interpreted the placement of the new corporate center as a threat to her business. However, instead of the challenge she originally saw, the corporate center offered her new opportunity.

ATTRACTING THE ELEMENTS FOR EXPANSION
Sybil was lucky. She didn't have to acquire more space for her business or find outside investors. Nor was she in the market for acquiring other people's businesses. Her spell for opening up to expansive opportunities may have taken a circuitous route, but it did involve only one thing: how she could augment her existing business herself.

There are many instances when this is not so straightforward. Sometimes you'll just want to find bigger office space *and* upgrade your office equipment so that you are able to take on more projects or more kinds of work. Even in personal goals, expansion can be a complicated process. If you start to enjoy a sport or hobby, the more you progress into it, the more you may want to invest in it—be it an investment of time, money, and/or resources.

POWER BUNDLES If you want to attract lots of different opportunities, you can use charms that are also known as power bundles. These are small pouches you make that act like magnets to attract the potential you desire. Whereas the charms introduced earlier work in conjunction with your energy to amplify or protect it, a power bundle can attract the energy you are trying to help expand, drawing from the outside world.

Making a power bundle is a creative process. The spell at the end of this chapter can guide you through the basics of attracting property or deals. In each one you need to choose certain objects or symbols that have personal meaning.

You can also make group power bundles, which is when you are in a venture with others and, as a group, you want to attract outside potential. I used this technique with two colleagues of mine recently. We had been involved in a joint creative project and it was time to take it out into the world—that is, to sell it somewhere. We already had interest from one or two sources, but we wanted to bring in as many offers and meet as many people as we could. Together, we each brought a power object to contribute to the bundle, and we added the necessary herbs. We used a green candle, and all restated our commitment to the project and our openness to seeing it through to its highest potential. Although we haven't yet sealed a deal, we've had a great deal of opportunity and are still "examining the catch."

Since you create them yourself, you can use power bundles as "psychic magnets" to attract almost anything you want. You don't have to have any results in mind, just the outcome. We did our power bundle for making the best deal possible. Since deals are structured in so many different ways, we're letting the universe give us a lot of choices. Each company or individual who has approached us has had different ideas as to how our deal could be made. We asked for choice; now we're getting it. Just be aware that patience and commitment is required on the follow-through process. It may take some time, but that way you can get it right.

SINGLE-MINDED EXPANSION When you have a single-minded purpose—needing more space or new investors or the desire to make acquisitions—you can perform spells directed to those goals. You'll find that these spells are similar to the spells for initiation in Chapter Three. The difference between spells for expansion and initiation is subtle but important. You need to respect that you are adding on to what already exists. For instance, when you want to put an addition on your house in your expansion spell, you need to represent your house as an element in your spell. A photograph of the house, the deed, or any existing symbol of your current house is needed in the spell. When you are simply trying to find a house, you don't have that element to deal with.

This may sound like metaphysical red tape. However, it really is an important point. Your spell acts like a blueprint that you send up to the universe, the loose instructions for your desired outcome. If you don't say that this space you want is for your home and not your office, you could end up with the wrong result.

My friend Joan did a spell for home office space. She is in PR and felt that she could easily work at home aided by her computer, copier, phone, and fax. Her spell specifications stated that she didn't want to look at what she called "unsightly" office equipment, so she assumed she was going to have to build an extra room onto her house. In error, she used a spell for finding the best location for her business rather than a spell to augment or rework her current home. The universe listened to her request for home office space that was aesthetically pleasing, and she unintentionally happened upon very inexpensive office space a friend of hers was renting in an old converted Victorian mansion a few miles from her home. While this wasn't what she had in mind, she thought it was the best she could do. The office she rented was an old bedroom and her business machines fit perfectly into its dressing room. Although it wasn't what she had envisioned, it technically fit the specs of her spell. Eventually I advised her to cast the spell again, this time using a spell to augment her own home's space. She claims that her spell gave her new eyes with which to see her home. She thought that there might be a way to redesign her second floor to incorporate a room to house the office equipment, like the dressing room in the Victorian house. With the help of an interior designer, she was able to knock a few walls down and convert a large linen closet into a place for her office equipment; she also created a small but separate work area off her bedroom. She was delighted to have the office space outside her house while the work was being done, and now she is cozily set up on her own terms in her own home.

This sort of thing happens all too often when you aren't clear to yourself and the universe that you are looking to build on what already exists. You *can* correct any errors and eventually achieve what you want, but it may take more time.

A client of mine did a spell to attract investors in her dance studio, but she used the spell in Chapter Three to attract investors instead of the spell to increase outside investment in her current enterprise. She received word that a long-forgotten grant proposal had been accepted—but the money was intended for her to choreograph original dances rather than paint the walls, replace the floor, and do the other improvements she was hoping to implement.

She wasn't upset at the results of her spell, but she was more careful next time.

Even in making acquisitions, buying other companies or property to add to your current venture, these spells can help you to attract the right holdings, the right mix, to complement what you already have. Spells are useful for attracting not only a good idea, but the right idea for you.

ACQUISITIONS AND DIVERSIFICATION The last spells for expanding your venture are spells for acquisitions and diversification. If you have met one goal and it is going smoothly, you may want to get into something else totally separate but parallel to your ongoing enterprise. Perhaps you want to add more to your plate. Diversification is extending your interests into disparate fields. Acquisition is the act of taking possession of something that already exists.

Diversification and acquisition seem to be such large words, implying a large process. You may not picture yourself in the market to buy a company or to move some of your holdings from silver to gold. You don't have to be RJR/Nabisco to participate in diversification and acquisitions. You have only to want to supplement your current venture (not desert it) and to nourish another, newer goal.

Again, like the above spells for attracting expansive energy to a current enterprise, these spells for diversification and expansion need to incorporate your current "holding," or the business or venture that is already established. Your current venture is like a ballast, and its presence is what gives you the steadiness and the power to attract new, separate ventures.

My friend Kit is an author who has always had two careers; she is also a very successful creative consultant. Since she enjoys creating businesses and seeing them grow, she decided to diversify even further. However, she knew that she couldn't handle running two businesses and still write her books without outside help. Always creative, she combined two spells: the first for attracting the right partners and the second, a spell to diversify.

In the spell for diversification, Kit used her current creative consultancy as the basis from which to work. She asked that a new business be born to parallel and augment but not overwhelm her already stable enterprise. The spells worked synchronistically. On an out-of-town consulting job, Liz met a woman who eventually became her partner. They were both consultants on different coasts, and both were looking to take on something new and different. They established a joint marketing venture in an area of mutual interest. This business is now in the early stages of manifestation and is showing signs of success. Liz did have to hire outside help to free herself from some of the time-consuming aspects of her current projects during the birth of her new enterprise. This took loosening her grip on both money and control, but the excitement of starting her new venture gave her the energy to do so.

To supplement the power of the diversification process, you can always use the spells in previous chapters. Spells for atmosphere, locations, personal power, and many more can help you with the beginning of every enterprise you start.

Acquisition is a similar but different process, since it implies that you are acquiring what is already set up. You can diversify your holdings by acquisition instead of starting an entirely new enterprise from the ground up.

The act of acquiring is simple; it is like going shopping. You need to keep focused on your goal, but you also need to consider various ways your goal can be fulfilled. Like an attraction spell, the spell for acquisition brings suitable options to you for your consideration. A power bundle can help you, too, but the spell itself will not only attract opportunities but will make you more open to them and more internally shrewd about which choice will be right.

SPELL BASICS

Spells for expansion always use the waxing moon but vary in their format and day of the week. If you want to do your own, use a plant and add something to it, usually a symbol of what you are trying to expand.

Spell for Recovery

COLOR: Orange or yellow
FLOWER: Anything of vibrant color
DAY OF THE WEEK: Sunday
TIME OF DAY: First hour of darkness
TIME OF THE MONTH: Waxing moon

Spell for Expansion

COLOR: Purple and green
DAY OF THE WEEK: Thursday
TIME OF DAY: Third hour of darkness
TIME OF THE MONTH: Waxing moon
HERBS: Borage, ginger, nuts

Spell for
RECOVERY

On a new moon,
light a yellow candle.
Place snapdragons or tulips in a vase with water.
Place some nuts in their casings before the candle.

SAY ALOUD:

The spark of passion glows,
my field is poised for growth,
as the knowledge of the past
brings me into the future,
I reopen my flow to the universe.
I call in the power of creation
and reconnect to it with ease.
My energy grows, my power glows,
life and light are with me.
I reemerge for the greater good
in a current of abundance.
So be it.
And so it is.

Eat the nuts, or take them out of their shells
and bury them in earth.

Spell to
INCREASE BUSINESS OPPORTUNITIES

On a Thursday during a waxing moon
and in the third hour of darkness,
light an orange or gold candle.
Place a plant and a glass of water
in front of the candle.
Place some poppy seeds in a vessel
made of a natural substance.
If you are building opportunities
for an existing business,
place an object representing the business (a business
card, stationery, or the like) next to the candle.

SAY ALOUD:

I call in the power of Jupiter
and the energy of manifestation.
I open the space for plentiful business opportunity
with which I create abundance and prosperity.
(Water the plant and place the poppy seeds
in the soil.)
I participate in the flow of infinite abundance.
I affirm I nurture all I sow.
With all intention for the greater good,
I say so be it.
And so it is.

Blow out the candle.
Care for the plant as long as it lives.

Spell to
EXPAND SPACE

On a Thursday during a waxing moon
and in the third hour of darkness,
light a purple candle and a green candle.
Place a large empty pot of soil
in front of the candle.
Place a small houseplant next to the soil
with a glass of water.
Place an object from the space you wish to expand
next to the candle.

SAY ALOUD:

Within the greater good,
I expand the earth on which I thrive.
I open to the elements to create the potential
to expand my space. I affirm I am open
to the possibility of expansion
in whatever form it takes.
(Transplant the small plant into the larger pot.)
My power nourishes all that thrives and more.
(Water the plant and then place the object
on the soil.)
This is done within the greater good.
So be it.
And so it is.

Blow out the candle.

POWER BUNDLES

Power bundles are best made on a waxing moon.
You can make your own pouches or buy them
as long as they are in the right color. To make them
with others, each person must contribute
a personal object and take a drink of water.

To attract property:

On a Friday, use a green cloth. Place a rock, some
peas, something of the color orange, and a personal
object that is precious to you in the center.
Light an orange candle.
Drink some water.
Sew up the cloth with yellow thread.

SAY ALOUD:

The power of the universe combines with
my personal potential to draw in the right property.

Let the candle burn as long as you like.

To attract a deal:

On a Wednesday, use a blue cloth.
Place some lavender and dill in the center.
Write down the subject of the deal
you wish to make on a white piece of paper,
sign your name(s),
and place it in the center of the cloth.
Add a personal object that represents
a good deal to you.
Light a blue candle.
Drink some water.
Sew up the cloth with green thread.

SAY ALOUD:

*I bless this charm with the power to attract
the best deal. I ask the universe to join with me
to attract all right potential.*

Let the candle burn as long as you like.
When they are no longer useful,
remove your personal objects
and throw away the remains.

Spell to
ATTRACT NEW INVESTORS

On a Friday during a waxing moon
and during the third hour of darkness,
light a green candle and a purple candle.
Place pink roses and snapdragons in a vase
with water. Place some nutmeg and ginger
in a natural vessel in front of the vase.
Place a symbol of your current enterprise
next to the candles.
Hold the ginger in your palm.

SAY ALOUD:

I conjure the fires of potential,
the winds of opportunity,
and the heartfelt desire to use earthly wealth
to replenish my venture.
(Sprinkle some nutmeg on the green candle.)
I ask that the forces of the universe
bring me appropriate contributions
and that I allow them to come to me
with ease and joy.
I trust this process is guided
by the gentle hand of Venus.
So be it.
And so it is.

Blow out the candles.
Keep the offerings next to the flowers
until they die.

Spell for
DIVERSIFICATION

On a Sunday during a waxing moon
and in the first hour of darkness,
light candles in each color:
yellow, orange, red, blue, purple, green, white.
Place a plant and a glass of water
in front of the candles. In a natural vessel,
place four kinds of nuts in their shells.
Place an object that represents your current
enterprise in front of the candles.

SAY ALOUD:

I bless the abundance that my creativity brings me
and I ask the power of the Sun to shed light
on new creations.
In the flow of the universe,
I add to my venture.
I open to new paths, and continue to
manifest abundance.
In the realm of right action,
I am open to the diversity of my own power.
So be it.
And so it is.

Water the plant.
Place one nut of each kind and the object
of your current enterprise in the plant.
Blow out the candles when you feel ready.

Spell for
ACQUISITION

On a Friday during a waxing moon
and in the first hour of darkness,
light a purple candle and a green candle.
Place some borage and balm of gilead
in a natural vessel in front of the candles.
Place your favorite flowers in a vase of water.
Next to the vase, place at least four different flowers.

SAY ALOUD:

I bless the abundance in my life
and enjoy the prosperity and creativity within it.
With the power of the universe
and the energy of the elements,
I add to this sacred base.
(Place the other flowers, one stem at a time,
into the vase.)
The fires of my courage grow,
the potential the earth offers expands,
the realm of ideas opens, and
the current of relationships flows.
I manifest right acquisition.
So be it.
And so it is.

Throw out the offering on the full moon.

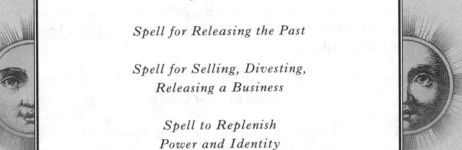

SEVEN

Spells for Change

I could probably write a whole book just about this topic. Change is one of the most feared processes in our lives, and it is the only thing we can count on. Nothing stays the same.

Some change is self-created, while other changes can come out of the blue, knocking the wind out of you. Either way, change is a part of life. Spell casting is a way of creating change or transformation consciously.

For the kind of change that appears out of the blue, the kind that can knock you down, spells can help to restore you to normalcy as well as heal any wounds that may have been created.

SUDDEN CHANGE

My client Lucy was terminated from her position without warning. She had been employed by a Wall Street firm that had a long-standing solid and profitable reputation. She came to me literally in a daze, trying to make sense out of this complete reversal in her career. She couldn't accept the idea that she was no longer employed. She had had an excellent review recently and had been promised a substantial promotion and raise. She kept reviewing the past events and could not find any way in which she could have seen this coming.

I met with her and she was in a bad state. Lucy couldn't stop trying to make sense of the events, or nonevents, leading up to her dismissal. This was a very nonproductive place for her. It was an inert state of shock, and there was no room for healing until she moved out of it. I gave Lucy a spell for surrender, so that instead of resisting the reality of her termination, she could succumb to it.

The spell for surrender is a gentle spell; it's like a psychic tranquilizer. It allows you to accept what is going on in a nonjudgmental way. Lucy surrendered to her dismissal and then realized she needed to cope with that issue. The feeling of loss and sadness overwhelmed her.

The Spell for Spaciousness and Tolerance (Chapter Five) was useful in order to restore her sense of self. In the interim, Lucy conversed with colleagues who had been similarly dismissed. She found that what she had believed to be a sound company with integrity and a sense of "doing the right thing" was not the reality. There had been political infighting and back-stabbing. She read the *Wall Street Journal* and learned that a scandal was brewing surrounding mismanaged funds. Lucy quickly had to dismantle her idea of the company she worked for and see it as it really was. Her belief and her vision had to be reconstructed. As soon as Lucy could see her company clearly, she was able to reconcile the fact that she didn't want to work in a place like that anyway. She no longer saw her termination as an incomprehensible act. As she adjusted her vision she was also able to gain perspective.

Lucy still loved her work and wanted to continue to work on Wall Street. She used a spell to replenish her power and identity just to keep her buoyant and positive. While other colleagues were still recovering from the shock and loss of position, Lucy used her spell to hold her belief in herself steady and went out to look for another job. She used a variety of spells from Chapter Two (Basic Spells for Success) and found a position within eight weeks of her termination.

Lucy's spells helped her reconnect to her power and avoid panicking. Sudden change can evoke the worst fears—and fear is a debilitating state. By immediately surrendering, Lucy created room to see the situation differently. This is not easy to do, but if you can keep your center in the face of unexpected change, you will be able to glide through it rather than be flattened by it.

The flow of change takes you with it, one way or another.

Sudden change can occur and does occur in all parts of our lives. It can be as simple as your dry cleaner going out of business or your air conditioner going on the blink. It doesn't have to be dramatic or life-threatening. There is no way of predicting sudden change—which is the chaotic "poetry" of the universe. Sudden change isn't always bad either. One day you could be handed a lottery ticket and the next day become a millionaire, or, more likely, you could receive good news or unexpected surprises. We don't usually see good luck as positive sudden change, but that is what it is.

SELF-CREATED CHANGE

Self-created change is gaining popularity in our society, but it is still nowhere near as exploited as it could be. Many of us avoid change, resisting even the most minor shifts in order to maintain a sense of security. Unfortunately, this sense of security is often an illusion—e.g., Lucy's vision of her so-called solid employer. Holding on to something hard is a good way of choking the life out of it, and it can blind you from opportunities outside of your current situation. Keeping your hand open allows different things to fall into it. Somewhere between the choke hold and the open hand is your personal balance. You can allow yourself to submit to change when necessary and, much more important, you can create change when you need it.

Change that you consciously bring about is the most interesting kind; it is an exploration you initiate, guide, and harvest on your own terms.

When I decided to change my career, I was challenged ferociously by some friends and colleagues. I didn't know what my new career would be, but I knew that I needed to make a great change. Those who opposed my decision were constantly pointing out that I was successful in advertising and that I "should" stay in it since there was no "reason" to change. There was great fear that I would fail on their part (not my fear, by the way) and there was a certain hostility in their reaction. It appeared to me that some people just didn't want me to rock the boat, that somehow changing my life threatened them. Why would it make any difference to anyone else if I failed or if I changed my career? I didn't realize it until much later, but my self-created change annoyed them; if I did it, why didn't they? Self-created change is not leaving well enough alone. It is going for the best you can get.

Although it is shifting, our culture still has a HUGE resistance to change even when change doesn't affect us directly. That is what I learned. If you are going to create change for yourself, be aware of this. You must be committed to your cause and know that there will be people who won't want you to do it or to succeed. You may need to gather a lot of energy to face this outside inertia, but if you are game, you have a shot at the brass ring.

SHEDDING THE PAST Before you make a large change, you are best off clearing away things you don't need from the past. If you've been reading this book attentively, you know by now that clearing precedes initiating, and in the process of change, it is no different. My friend Donna likens it to a snake shedding its skin. In order to move into a new life or a new part of your life, you have to let go of the old one. Chances are, you've outgrown it anyway.

Here I must warn you. If you are going to undertake a large-scale change, don't do it lightly. It isn't possible. Any large shift takes time and patience and a certain amount of shedding. Like a snake, once the skin has been shed, you can't get back into it.

Not all change is gargantuan. You don't have to transform your entire life. The spells in this chapter are good for all kinds of self-created change; shedding is part of it, too. No matter what, going toward something new means shifting away, leaving something old behind.

Dale wanted to sell his manufacturing business over three years ago. He was trying to downshift his business life, since he was approaching his sixties and wanted to try his hand at a few other ventures before really thinking about retirement. Dale's firm had done very well. He wanted to sell it for a certain amount of money so that he could pursue his other interests with financial ease. He let it be known that he was ready to sell and started working with his bank to shop for buyers.

Although there was a lot of interest at first, prospects dropped off. In each case, there was some deal point that didn't work out. Discouraged, Dale came to me for a consultation. I told him that he needed to do a spell for releasing his business. He had started the company and it was his "baby"; I sensed he wasn't really dealing with the emotional side of selling it. Dale argued with me, telling me that it was the market, the bank, anything but him in the way of a deal. I finally convinced him to humor me and had him promise to perform the spell for releasing.

Not long after we met, he was back. He said that he had done the spell and that he was now feeling afraid; perhaps he didn't want to sell his business after all. We discussed his fear and found there was an underlying concern that he was going to lose his power. This is a very common "spell hangover," especially in a releasing spell. The psychic hold Dale had on his business was tied to his own identity. Unconsciously he didn't want to sell his business because it would leave him without a job, a title, a place in the world; Dale's power was held within his company and not in himself.

The quick fix to that problem is the Spell to Replenish Power and Identity. Dale's spell helped him create a broader identity and one that he found more attractive than his old one. He started to see himself as an investor and entrepreneur instead of a manufacturer.

Once his attitude changed, he was more willing to let go of his business. His spell worked to give him more energy to break through his own ambivalence. After a few fits and starts, Dale sold his business within a year.

THE SHADOW SIDE OF CHANGE

Instigating change can bring about many unforeseen circumstances. They aren't always negative either, but those unpleasant side effects are the ones we always remember. This is called the shadow side, or the unconscious side of change. When our natural flow is asked to shift—whether by choice or not—we may shake up some very important security issues and hence arouse uncomfortable emotions. The following is the basic sampler of what usually comes up from the shadow.

1. FEAR Any change can bring about fear. Dale's unconscious fear was linked to his identity in the business world, which happened to be a very important element in his life. A smaller change may seem pretty safe, but you'd be surprised at how much fear can arise just by changing routine. Fear naturally arises in changing situations, whether it be conscious or unconscious. You can use the Spell for Releasing or Softening Fear in Chapter Two whenever you like. Since the world offers us change on a constant basis, fear can easily become a daily experience.

The fear that accompanies more profound changes in your life can sometimes be a little overwhelming. Fear can appear in many ways. If it gets too much, you may want to perform the Spell for Surrender, which is like the Spell for Handing Over Despair (Chapter Five). In this spell, you surrender to the forces of change and ask them to guide you to a safe place. This spell takes the edge off overwhelming fear and can give you a reprieve from worry.

2. CONFLICT AND ANGER The effect of change,

leaving things out of balance for a while before equilibrium is restored, can make some of us downright cranky. I've seen people manifest the most amazing conflicts, completely unconsciously, as part of the change they are making. Norm, an old friend from advertising, decided he wanted to start his own agency and leave the big corporate world behind. He lined up the financing, found partners, and was ready to resign. Instead, he picked a huge fight with his boss, then his boss's boss, and as a result, got fired. He didn't realize that he created the conflict in order to help him with his change. Instead, he got completely carried away by a minor creative issue, which really didn't matter since he was planning to leave. Norm's anger, an unanticipated reaction to his own desire for change, manifested unconsciously. He is not happy that he departed under such unpleasant circumstances and sees now that it was unnecessary. I contend that Norm didn't know how to leave or how to say he was leaving without an excuse, so he created one. As an afterthought to clean it up, Norm did a spell to release the past. He made peace both within himself and with his ex-colleagues.

Anger can come up even in seemingly insignificant changes. I speak for myself, here. I changed my furniture around, but when I come in, I still dump my mail and keys on the floor—*where the table used to be*—and then I become furious. Months can go by and I will still forget that I changed things around. This absentmindedness is a symptom of yet another shadow side of change: inner conflict.

3. INNER CONFLICT—RESISTANCE If you have taken the pains to create a change in your life and you are working hard to stay with the flow of it, you may find it gets bumpy here and there. That is normal, since change takes you out of sync with the world for a while, as if you are in between gears. Just pay attention to what you do have influence over and how you handle it. Since change is a multistep process and could involve almost every spell in

this book, there will be many places for you to choose how to handle yourself. If you start to feel like you are becoming a victim, you may have uncovered a little resistance to change. My pathetic habit of dropping my mail on the floor is definitely a symptom of resisting the way my furniture is placed. I have to really examine if it is what I want after all. That is what resistance does; it forces you to be clear about your intention and goal. If you don't believe in it, why should anyone else? Again, the Spell for Surrender is a great help when you are encountering your own resistance to change. It can help you refocus on the goal, not the process.

When my friend Stacy changed careers from selling antiques to publishing, she had to get used to the corporate office aesthetic. She was not happy. Even though she wanted to work in publishing more than anything, she just found fault with everything from the architecture to the ladies' room. She had made her change, but she really resisted being happy in it. She did the Spell for Surrender and gave herself some time. Eventually, the world of publishing was so colorful and vibrant that she stopped noticing the ugly file cabinets and tiny office spaces. Her spell helped her remove the narrowness of resistance so she could refocus and shift away from her old work with visual beauty and move into the world of intellectual beauty.

4. SADNESS Change is definitely a place that brings up sadness, and no one likes to be reminded of it. It is easy to understand that change you didn't plan on could make you sad, like losing a job. It's when you've made the change entirely consciously that you may not have planned on feeling a loss. It happens and it is completely natural. Lots of people cry at their going-away parties, even when they are moving on to better things. In the metaphysical viewpoint, change is simply transformation that brings you into a large place; it doesn't dismiss or nullify your past experience, it adds to it. Yet our experience with change is so unpracticed and feared that we simply

don't see it that way. Don't be surprised if sadness comes up and let it flow through you.

For all shadow effects of change, it is very important that you allow yourself to feel them. If you don't, you'll just let them build up until they burst. The Spell for Surrender will help ease the flow and you can do any of the clearing spells in the preceding chapters to help you along.

THE BIG LEAP: HOW TO USE AND SUSTAIN RISK

Sometimes the change you want to make can seem out of reach. Your goal will probably manifest in a way you least expect, and it could take more time or resources than you had counted on. You may get cold feet and want to give up. Once you are in the change process, however, it is very hard, if not impossible, to turn back. This is where it gets tricky. There is a leap of faith involved in almost every change, and somehow you'll have to find the strength and courage within yourself to take that leap.

When my friend Sandy decided to move into the city after five years of establishing his massage therapy business in a small town, he went through a classic leap of faith. His change was self-created. He looked for adequate space in which to work and live; he began to do spells for attracting clients and for adjusting his social life. He did everything possible to make his change graceful and seamless. However, the universe didn't come up with enough clients in enough time for Sandy to feel he had made the right move. He began to doubt the decision after it was too late—he had moved and invested both time and money in this change. That is when risk presents itself in its purest form—when it is too late to go back. Sandy was beside himself. He had to make a choice as to how he was going to deal with this. He saw three options: go into debt using credit cards, borrow money from his parents, or bail out altogether and go back to where he started.

Sandy had to evaluate his options with a clear head, so he first did the Spell for Spaciousness and Tolerance (Chapter Five), which eased his nerves, and then he did the Spell for Clarity (Chapter Four). Both spells took some of the immediate pressure off of him. He came to the conclusion that he undertook this move on his own without help and wanted to continue with it. That ruled out borrowing or bailing. Now Sandy had to face drawing money off his credit until he was again more affluent. This is where a spell for using and sustaining risk is effective.

Sandy didn't want to accumulate too much debt, but he knew he needed money to live. He did the spell and took out a sizable cash advance without fear attached to it. A spell for using risk acts like a protective coating on the risk itself—you don't want to go into a risk situation loaded with fear, for instance. Sandy's spell allowed him to see the act of borrowing money as a positive investment, and also reignited his courage and faith in himself. Thus, he undertook his risk with positive energy, which helps it work out.

In almost all types of change, there is that final moment when you have to really commit or recommit yourself to your ideal. It is particularly difficult to do when you are fearful that things won't work out. Fear will keep you from investing power into your risk, which can cripple efficacy.

This leap of faith in the area of risk is linked to surrender, and the two spells work well together.

YES, IT REALLY IS WORTH IT

If you started out with a fear of change, I'm not sure I've done anything to alleviate it. I have taken pains to show you the shadow side of change and the constant need to take a leap of faith and face risk. You're probably sitting there thinking "Why bother?"

Because it's worth it, that's why. There is nothing better than going after a heartfelt goal and seeing it become a reality. There is no bigger rush of energy than watching a dream come true. You can do it. I don't think I ever said it would be easy, but it is worth it.

The more skillful you are at facing and creating change in your life, the less fear you will have and, again, more power from that. Your abundance, prosperity, and fulfillment can grow exponentially when you have the experience of transforming your world.

Even though the process can have its painful moments, it is worth it. You'll never have to wonder "what if?"

SPELL BASICS

These are the basic instruments for the magic of change and transformation. You can devise your own spells if you so desire, using these elements.

COLOR: White and one of your favorite colors
FLOWER: White flowers and whatever is
your favorite flower
DAY OF THE WEEK: Sunday or any new moon for
beginnings
Saturday or a full moon for
endings
TIME OF DAY: After sunset

For major changes, do the Spell for Releasing the Past on the full moon when the sun is in the sign opposite your own (see chart following) and on the summer solstice, June 21.

To create the new passageway for a major change, do the Spell to Start an Enterprise (Chapter Three) on the new moon when the sun is in your birth sign and on the winter solstice, December 21.

Your Sign	*Dates in Which the Full Moon Should Fall*	
Aries	9/23–10/22	(Libra)
Taurus	10/23–11/21	(Scorpio)
Gemini	11/22–12/20	(Sagittarius)
Cancer	12/21–1/19	(Capricorn)
Leo	1/20–2/17	(Aquarius)
Virgo	2/18–3/19	(Pisces)
Libra	3/20–4/19	(Aries)
Scorpio	4/20–5/20	(Taurus)
Sagittarius	5/21–6/20	(Gemini)
Capricorn	6/21–7/22	(Cancer)
Aquarius	7/23–8/22	(Leo)
Pisces	8/23–9/22	(Virgo)

Spell for
RELEASING THE PAST

On a Saturday during a waning moon
and in the second hour of darkness,
light a white candle.
Place white lilies in a vase with water.
Place some sage and lavender in a natural vessel
next to the vase.
Place an onion in its skin next to the candle.

SAY ALOUD:

In the peace and space of the fading moon
and with the finality of Saturn's hand,
I release that which has passed and holds no power
in the future.
I release negativity and invoke protection,
that which must be shed finds its way back to its origin.
I release the past and open to the future.
(Peel the skin off the onion.)
I do this with faith in infinite abundance
and bless the path in front of me.
I release my past to the universe and say
so be it.
And so it is.

Blow out the candle. Throw the onion skin out.
Dispose of the sage when the flowers die.
Use the onion in cooking.

Spell for
SELLING, DIVESTING, RELEASING
A BUSINESS

On a Tuesday during a waning moon
and in the first hour of darkness,
light a white candle and a green candle.
Place some yellow roses in a vase with water.
Place cinnamon, cloves, and ginger in a vessel
made of a natural substance.
Write the name of what you are selling
on a white piece of paper.

SAY ALOUD:

With gratitude for the abundant road I walk,
I ask the universe to join me in releasing my venture.
I affirm the power of this manifestation
and allow it to thrive outside of my domain.
This release is pure and clear in intention
and draws opportunity and abundance in its wake.
I release this for the greater good
and ask that it find its right place in the world.
With the fire of Mars, I let this go.
(Burn the paper.)
In fire, the release is pure.
So be it.
And so it is.

Blow the candles out and throw the ashes away
outside your domain.
Throw the herbs out when the flowers are dead.

Spell to
REPLENISH POWER AND IDENTITY

On a Sunday during a waxing moon
and in the third hour of darkness,
light a candle in your favorite color.
Place carnations in a vase with water.
In a natural vessel,
place a bay leaf and some saffron
Next to the candles, place a personal object
that brings enjoyment and pride.

SAY ALOUD:

*In the healing of the Sun
and the life-giving light it gives,
I claim my strength and identity.*
(Close your eyes and visualize sunlight.
Breathe it in.)
*I reconnect with the universal flow of all power
and do this for the greater good.*
(Continue to breathe in light
until you feel complete.)
*So be it.
And so it is.*

Blow out the candle.
Dispose of the herbs at the full moon.

Spell for
SURRENDER

On any evening during a waning moon,
light a white candle and a yellow candle.
Place a plant and a glass of water
in front of the candles.

SAY ALOUD:

The mysterious flow of the universe is ever creative.
As my life force reconnects and re-forms
with infinite abundance and possibility,
I release my hold on what has been
and surrender to what will be.
I trust the guardians to support me through this time,
through my own fire, earth, air, and water.
The unknown holds hope, light, and possibility,
and I am open to its pulse.
I affirm my faith in myself and the universe
and say so be it.
And so it is.

Water the plant.
Let the candles burn until you feel complete.

Spell to
USE AND SUSTAIN RISK

On a Thursday during a waxing moon
and during the third hour of darkness,
light a green candle.
Place yellow roses in a vase with water.
Place orange peel and balm of gilead in a vessel
made of a natural substance.

SAY ALOUD:

Lucky Jupiter, in your day and hour,
I ask that you join me in grounding
the manifestation of my risk for the greater good.
I affirm my flow is connected to the universe
and that I breathe with patience and tolerance
as the process of abundance unfolds.
I offer my faith and power to ensure the outcome.
I turn this over to the universe with trust.
So be it.
And so it is.

Blow out the candle.
Dispose of the offering on the full moon.

AFTERWORD

Your success is a function of your own creativity, power, and willingness to take an active role in forming your life. It's not all that complicated. With these spells, you'll realize just how much influence you have in making things happen.

It is especially important that you learn this now. Our world is shifting away from a materially driven culture and this shift is going to bring you more choice. Take time to really consider what is important to you and assess how much you have of it in your life now. These spells can help you amplify the pleasure you take in what already exists as well as help you create new paths to fulfillment. You just need to open yourself up to your own potential, the magic you can create with it.

You can use these spells in any situation, no matter how mundane. As soon as you begin to hook up to the flow of your own creativity, you'll see results.

Magic is all around you, possibility just waiting to happen. I wish you great energy to manifest your success, whatever your heart's desire. And may it be a long and ever-evolving dance with abundance, prosperity, and happiness.

APPENDIX

CHARM MAKING AND POWER BUNDLES FOR BEGINNERS

Some of the spells in this book call for making charms and power bundles. These are objects you make and "charge" with a certain energy. Carrying the object with you gives you that charge.

Charms can be very powerful, but it is important that you follow instructions and use them only for what they were intended. The charms you make are really for you alone, but if you make one for someone else, you need to have them "claim" it. This requires some participation in the charm-making process, either in choosing the herbs or in claiming aloud that the charm is theirs and they are open to its power.

To make a charm, you may use any ordinary cloth and thread. You will place certain ingredients on the cloth and then sew it up. It is easiest to start with a large piece of cloth and, when it is time to stitch it up, sew inside the perimeter of the cloth. You can cut away any excess cloth. As you sew, using loose, basting stitches, you are creating a drawstring effect. When you're finished, you can cinch the thread tightly to make a little bag. Wrap the thread around the neck of the bag and push the needle through the center before knotting it.

Do not use silk or nonbreathing fabrics for your charms. Cotton and wool work nicely. You can also purchase charm bags, like jewelry pouches. Again, stay away from silk.

DISPOSING OF SPELL MATERIALS

The only spell ingredients that don't have longevity are herbs. These should be thrown out or put in plants, which return them to the earth.

Gems can be cleared and used again for something else. To clear them, hold them over smoldering sage (in the smoke) or soak them in saltwater made from sea salt.

Candles can be used for other spells as long as you have a conscious intention for their next use. Clear them simply by blowing out the flame with the intention that your spell is complete. If you forget to clear them, they could carry with them the magic of the last spell. This usually doesn't produce negative results, but it is always best to clear everything when you're done.

Flowers can be allowed to wilt and die on their own time. Throw them out when they are dead.

Charms and power bundles should be destroyed when they have served their purpose. It is best to create new ones each time you need one. Destroy them by throwing them away.

Anything else you have used should be consciously cleared or returned to the earth. If you've
used a photograph or personal effect, you may want
to release it from your spell simply by shaking it
back into its original form. You can shake a photograph like a thermometer and it will shake off your
spell energy.

INDEX